LMS
LOCOMOTIVE PROFILES

No. 9 – MAIN LINE DIESEL-ELECTRICS Nos. 10000 and 10001

by
DAVID HUNT

WILD SWAN PUBLICATIONS

Between May and September 1950 the two diesels worked the up 'Royal Scot' and down Euston–Glasgow sleeping car express. They are seen in this photograph passing Apsley with 10001 leading and coupled with their No. 2 ends adjacent to each other, which was the normal way they worked in multiple. By this time, the silver roofs were distinctly grey but the locomotives were still kept clean.
FOX PHOTOS

No. 9 – MAIN LINE DIESEL-ELECTRICS Nos. 10000 and 10001

INTRODUCTION

Just over three weeks before the end of the LMS, the CME, H. G. Ivatt, drove the first diesel locomotive built for regular main-line service on a British railway out of the paint shop at Derby Works.[1] It had been a race against time to ensure that No. 10000 entered service under LMS auspices and by the time it became the property of British Railways, the engine had amassed 537 miles running. The large cast-aluminium alloy letters firmly riveted to the body sides left onlookers in no doubt as to who was responsible for its construction and although the diesel engine, generators, traction motors and control gear were manufactured by the English Electric Company, the locomotive frames, body, bogies and other mechanical equipment were designed by LMS draughtsmen and built at Derby Works. Therefore, No.10000 and the other member of the class, 10001, which appeared seven months later, can rightly be described as LMS locomotives. They can also be described as principal products of the CME Department's last great project and went on to have a substantial influence on the future motive power of British Railways. For these and many other reasons, the publisher of the *LMS Locomotive Profiles* series of monographs felt that that they merited attention and asked me if I would prepare a volume about them. Since I, too, found the subject an interesting one, I had no hesitation in agreeing and was delighted to find that there were several drawings of the locomotives in the national archive held at the National Railway Museum as well as some sketches and other primary material in the possession of friends and colleagues.

In keeping with the principle now established through previous works in the *LMS Locomotive Profile* series, I hope to give some idea of the reasons for the conception and design of the LMS main-line diesel-electrics as well as a brief description of their construction and service. Since they were such a radical departure from what had gone before, however, I feel that we need to examine briefly the reasons for, and history of, the adoption of diesel traction on the LMS in order to understand properly why and how they came about. In my view, this in turn requires a short essay into the development of the diesel locomotive globally and nationally. The subject, however, is extremely long and involved and there isn't room or, I feel, necessity in this volume to do more than scratch the surface. Therefore I have tried to précis the main points in the context of Nos. 10000 and 10001. Similarly, I feel that something needs to be written about their place in British locomotive history as they had an undoubted influence on

No. 10000 is shown here at an unknown location shortly after entering service and certainly before August 1948 when it entered Derby Works. After that time it had stiffening webs on the bogie side plates and the oval boiler access panels on its body sides were blanked off. E. WOODS

subsequent British Railways traction policy and design. Again, though, this story is complex and I have only tried to summarise what I consider to be the main points.

When writing about diesel locomotives, we have to be careful regarding nomenclature. Whilst it can be argued that the 'engine' of a steam locomotive consists purely of the cylinders and valve gear, it is more common to use 'engine' and 'locomotive' as interchangeable terms for the whole machine. When writing about diesel locomotives, however, I feel that in order to avoid confusion the word 'engine' should be used only to denote the power plant that drives the locomotive through electrical or mechanical transmission. Throughout this book, therefore, I will be using the term 'engine' purely when referring to the diesel power plant and 'locomotive' to mean the entire machine. I will also be using 'diesel' or 'diesel engine', with a small 'd', in its modern context to embrace all high-pressure compression-ignition engines rather than just the type developed by Rudolf Diesel.

In preparing this volume, I have received a great deal of help from a number of people. Principal among them is my good friend Bob Meanley, Chief Engineer at Tyseley Locomotive Works Ltd., who has provided me with anecdotes and information without which many questions would have remained unanswered. Bob also put me in touch with other sources of material as well as reading through the first draft and correcting mistakes. Invaluable assistance has been forthcoming from the staff of the National Railway Museum, in particular from Martin Bashforth, who has provided me with copies of the most useful drawings we have found there, Helen Ashby, Head of Knowledge and Collections, and Phil Atkins, who is the Research Centre Manager and has an almost encyclopaedic knowledge of locomotive history. I must also thank four people with first-hand knowledge of the locomotives who have given me invaluable help, namely my friend and co-author of other books Fred James, David Russell, Dennis Monk and Peter Meredith. Peter was a fitter in Derby Works who later became an inspector on diesel-electrics and was closely involved with the locomotives both when they were being built and subsequently in service. The other three gentlemen were all apprentices at Derby Works, Fred being an electrical fitter by late 1947 and involved with the locomotives' construction. Dennis was undergoing his apprenticeship whilst the twins were being built and later became a mechanical inspector at Derby, being involved with the locomotives virtually all through their lives. David started his apprenticeship in 1954, and worked in the diesel shop when 10000 and 10001 underwent their lengthy repairs in 1956 as described later. He subsequently had considerable influence on the design of many of the last diesel locomotive classes built for operation on British Railways. Through the late David Tee, I have also had access to some correspondence and notes from Eric Langridge, whose section in Derby Locomotive Drawing Office was responsible for a considerable portion of the design. Much-appreciated assistance in gathering material has also been forthcoming from David Jarman, Product Engineer at Preston for Alstom Transport Service, Ron Jones, an ex-service engineer with GEC Traction and Alstom, and one of my co-authors in other works, John Jennison. My good friend Adrian Tester has given advice on some engineering matters and in my search for suitable photographs I have had assistance from many people who are acknowledged in the captions. Two gentlemen, however, have gone to great lengths to help in this respect and so I must single out Nick Wheat and David Hills for special thanks.

Despite all this assistance, there is, no doubt, a plethora of errors and omissions in what I have written and for that I offer my apology. I hope, however, that readers with more or better information, particularly personal experience, will contact me by post via Wild Swan Publications, through the web site at *midlandrecord.com* or by e-mail to *dvhunt@aol.com* so that their wisdom can be passed on in the 'Further Information' column of *LMS Journal*.

Sometime between returning to LMR main-line working in April 1955 and being taken into Derby Works for heavy repair in January 1956, No. 10000 was photographed with a down express just south of Hademore crossing and water troughs between Tamworth and Lichfield Trent Valley. It wore the smaller 'monocycling lions' that it received in February 1954 and had the later Southern Region 6P 5FA power classification.
HOULSON COLLECTION, CTY. E. M. JOHNSON

No. 9 – MAIN LINE DIESEL-ELECTRICS Nos. 10000 and 10001

ORIGINS

The origins of the LMS main-line diesel-electric locomotives really go back to pre-Grouping days – in fact, to the earliest days of the public railway – and can be summed up in one word – economy. Some written works seem to suggest that the need for economy was a phenomenon first appearing in the post-Grouping or even post-war railways but that was far from being the case. The very factors that gave rise to the public railway as a viable venture were economic and from the establishment of the Stockton and Darlington there was always a need to economise in some way. A few examples will suffice to illustrate this. Take, for instance, the change from iron to steel for both locomotive tyres and rails around 1860; the benefits included a reduction in rolling resistance, more even wear on tyres – which also resulted in less resistance to motion and hence less strain on components – and longer lives for tyres and rails. Steel, however, was more expensive to produce but the overall economic benefit from reduced wear and lower maintenance costs was massive and there was a collateral, albeit slight, effect of reduced coal consumption. The change from green to crimson lake paint for Midland locomotives in the 1880s was simply an economy measure as the latter was less fugitive a colour and engines consequently did not need repainting as often. Superheating, often thought of by enthusiasts as introduced to improve locomotive performance, was seen by railway managers around the turn of the century primarily as a way of using less coal and water, which outweighed the extra cost of construction and maintenance. The list is almost endless but the foregoing will suffice to illustrate the process.

Whilst these points can seem fairly obvious as far as using less materials and consumables is concerned, there were also savings that resulted from reduced manpower requirements. In the 19th and first years of the 20th centuries, the latter was not as significant as it was later to become. By the time the carnage of the first world war was over, however, it was exercising the minds of those in charge of Britain's railways and at the Grouping it was obvious that future plans for running the railways must begin to address the question of manpower costs. When it came to labour needs, few things were more demanding than the steam locomotive. Many avenues about which others and I have written were explored to reduce the dependency of the prime movers on a vast army of people to keep them running. Such things as the progressive repair system, better springing, improved valve gear, mechanical coaling plants and many more economised in manpower either directly, by requiring less people to do a particular job, or indirectly by reducing maintenance and repair effort.

Each conventional steam locomotive also needed two men to operate it and thoughts on the LMS turned towards cost reduction through single-man operation in two particular areas, the first being branch line, or short-distance, passenger traffic. The pre-Grouping companies had made several attempts to introduce steam railmotors on various lines but none was really successful. Electrification on LMS constituents proved worthwhile as early as 1904 when the L&YR electrified the Liverpool–Southport commuter line and other companies followed suit on some intensively worked routes.[2] For secondary routes and minor branch lines, however, the enormous initial expense and maintenance costs of electrification made it unsuitable. An alternative appeared to be some sort of internal combustion-engined vehicle. In 1910, General Electric in America produced a petrol railcar, after which the idea spread and in 1913 British Westinghouse began building a petrol-electric version, one of which was bought by the L&NWR; it was not a tremendous success. After the Grouping, the LMS tried a few experiments with modified motor buses and pneumatic-tyred railbuses but none of those was really successful either. The declining economic climate of the 1920s made the search for savings more imperative and since internal combustion hadn't yet answered the company's needs, a trial of a Sentinel two-cylinder, chain-driven steam railcar commenced in 1926. Initial impressions were favourable and led to the purchase of twelve of them the following year but wider use brought less satisfaction and all had gone by the end of 1937.[3]

Development of the diesel engine and its application to railway use had been progressing during this time and had reached the stage where it seemed to offer advantages for the sort of traffic under consideration. In 1927, therefore, the company began looking at diesel-powered railcars and multiple units. A short while later, the Chairman of the LMS, Josiah Stamp, stipulated that a need existed for 'more economical shunting units' and in 1929 a joint working party from the staffs of both the Superintendent of Motive Power and the CME was set up to examine the requirement.[4] Sir Henry Fowler was at that time CME and his representative on the working part was his Chief Technical Assistant, T. F. Hornbuckle. The latter had a reputation for original thinking and soon identified that potentially the most worthwhile avenue for investigation was single-manned locomotives. Consideration was given to such things as adapted road vehicles, petrol engines, oil engines, and oil or automatic coal firing of steam locomotives.[5] Of all the options, however, diesel power seemed the most promising, although it was several years before the LMS got around to applying it.

It is probably worthwhile at this stage considering briefly some of the reasons for adopting diesel power. As with any form of internal combustion engine, it had the advantage over steam that the fuel could be turned off when the locomotive was idle between trips or shunting turns. Compared with other forms of power production, the thermal efficiency (the ability to convert fuel into work) was high, being above 30% compared with the steam engine's 6–7% and about 10% for the petrol engine. The disadvantages when compared with petrol engines included the fact that the diesels' much higher compression ratios – typically 20:1 as opposed to 8:1 – meant that they were heavier and costlier to produce. The former, however, was not really considered a particular disadvantage in the context of shunting locomotives with their requirement for adhesive weight. The maximum RPM of diesels was lower and their effective RPM band smaller than petrol engines, so they required more sophisticated transmission systems. They also needed fuel injection, which was expensive and, in the early days, less reliable than carburettors, as well as requiring a lot of maintenance. However, they tended to last longer than petrol engines, needed far less disposal and preparation time, and could carry enough fuel for up to a week's work without having to spend valuable time filling up. These factors, together with their much greater fuel economy, potentially outweighed the drawbacks.

The compression-ignition engine was the subject of two patents taken out by a German engineer, Dr. Rudolf Diesel, in 1892 and sold the following year to a consortium operated by Maschinenfabrik Augsburg-Nürnberg (MAN) and Krupps. After considering gas, petroleum and even pulverised coal as fuels, Diesel designed his engine to run on vegetable oil. The first prototype built by MAN under Diesel's supervision in the summer of 1893 was not functional but the second one was and managed an efficiency of 16.6% by the summer of 1894 running on peanut oil. Towards the end of 1896 and early in 1897, the third prototype, sometimes referred to as the 'first Diesel engine', became truly functional using heavy fuel oil. Nowadays this is more commonly known as paraffin, the petroleum industry having realised that a fraction of its own product could be utilised and promoted the idea in consequence. In 1898, Diesel withdrew from further work on the compression-ignition engine and MAN continued the development.

At the same time, similar engines were also being developed in England by William Priestman and Herbert Ackroyd-Stuart. The latter took out a patent for an oil engine in 1890 and sold it to Hornsby of Grantham. The first examples were spark and then bulb-ignition but later ones employed compression-ignition. Although compression-ignition engines are generally known today as 'diesels', Priestley's and Ackroyd-Stuart's work had a more direct and important bearing on development of the modern high-compression units than did Rudolf Diesel's.

Because the first ones were large and heavy and had a low effective RPM range, diesel engines were initially used in stationary machines. In 1903 the application was extended to ships and, with support from the MAN Company, to French submarines in 1904. In 1906 a diesel engine was used to power a motor lorry but it wasn't until the 1920s that they began to gain wider acceptance in vehicle manufacture and by the mid-1930s were fitted to motor buses in Germany. In 1936, Daimler-Benz unveiled their first diesel car.

The earliest use of diesel engines in railway vehicles seems to have been in 1896 when Hornsby & Sons of Grantham produced the first of six narrow-gauge Hornsby-Ackroyd engined shunters for use at Woolwich Arsenal and Chatham Dockyard. Production of these machines ended in 1903 and while they were being built, Tom Hornbuckle was serving his apprenticeship at the factory. In 1912, a large 1,200 hp direct drive diesel locomotive was built by Sulzer and Borsig in Germany but it was a failure. The next reference I can find to a diesel locomotive is one made in 1918 by General Electric in America for the Jay St. Connecting Railroad in New York. Although it was not particularly successful, sufficient interest was generated for another, much more effective, diesel locomotive demonstrator to be produced in 1924 by the Schenectady Locomotive Works of the American Locomotive Company. It was powered by a 300hp Ingersoll-Rand diesel engine and fitted with General Electric generating and transmission equipment. Later the same year, General Electric and the American Locomotive Company co-operated in marketing production diesel shunters.

It was soon found that their maintenance costs were lower than equivalent steam locomotives per hour in service, fuel costs were lower, and they required fewer stops to replenish fuel and water reserves. Their day-to-day maintenance needs were also much less, which increased their availability.

The diesel engine itself was also undergoing a quantum improvement at this time, made possible largely by the work of Alan Chorlton in England and Robert Bosch in Germany, who were instrumental in the evolution of airless fuel injection. This led to the production of lighter, faster running and more powerful engines and broadened the scope for diesel traction on rails. By the time the LMS came to consider the best form of power for its shunting requirements in the late 1920s and early 1930s, these factors were well known. In February 1932, the Hunslet Engine Co. of Leeds demonstrated an 0-6-0 diesel-mechanical shunter at the British Industries Fair and later at the Waterloo Main colliery near Leeds. It then ran an eleven-week series of trials on the LMS, mainly on shunting duties but also involving a couple of trips on the main line from Leeds to Bradford with a brake van to assess its riding at higher speeds. Performance, reliability and convenience of this locomotive were impressive and effectively discounted all forms of traction other than diesel for shunting. It was also seen as extremely promising for other duties.

Having decided on diesel traction, the question then arose as to which method of transmission best suited the job. There were basically three options – diesel-mechanical, diesel-hydraulic and diesel-electric.[6] At the time, mechanical transmission systems could only handle relatively low power with any reliability and for anything above about 180 hp, one of the other methods had to be used. The first trial for branch passenger traffic actually pre-dated the Hunslet episode described above and was initiated by converting the old Bury to Holcombe Brook line four-car electric set to diesel-electric traction at Horwich Works in 1928.[7] It was powered by a 500 hp Beardmore diesel engine with English Electric generator and traction motors and entered service in July that year on the Preston–Blackpool line, At the time, Alan Chorlton, mentioned earlier in the context of airless fuel injection development, worked for the Beardmore Group in Glasgow. The firm was a world leader in the production of the new generation of lightweight diesel engines and had an international reputation for quality. It is somewhat surprising, therefore, that after only nine months the train was withdrawn following several failures and the engine returned to Beardmore. An LMS report into the trial stated that although there were savings in running costs when compared with a steam train of similar capacity, the interest charges due to high initial cost as well as the heavy renewal and maintenance penalties resulted in an overall loss. Beardmore proposed a further trial with modified equipment but the report concluded that, 'The time is not opportune for further trials,' and the firm's offer was turned down.[8]

The next appearance of diesel-electric vehicles on LMS metals was in 1933 when two privately built and owned single-car units were tried. One was constructed with a 200 hp engine by English Electric at the Dick, Kerr works in Preston and operated over various parts of the railway; the other was one of three demonstration 250 hp units built by Armstrong Whitworth at Scotswood with a Sulzer engine and traction motors on one bogie that ran between Euston and the British industries Fair at Castle Bromwich under Shell sponsorship. Both were carried on four-wheel bogies and seem to have been successful machines but neither was bought by the LMS.

No. 9 – MAIN LINE DIESEL-ELECTRICS Nos. 10000 and 10001

Also appearing in 1933 were three lightweight, 95 hp diesel-hydraulic, four-wheel railcars built by Leyland. Initial impressions of them were favourable but the four-wheel layout and relatively flimsy lightweight construction caused operating problems and they later became unreliable. Despite this, they lasted long enough to reach Nationalisation but didn't have any notable impact on LMS traction policy.

The previously-mentioned working party that was looking into the whole question of shunting locomotives reported in October 1931 that, 'The cost of the electrical equipment puts up the capital cost to such extent that it is difficult to make a case out for the adoption of the diesel-electric.' Consequently, the first experimental shunting locomotive, which was built at Derby Works utilising the frames of an old Midland Railway 0-6-0 tank engine No. 1831 and entered service in December 1932, was a 400 hp example with hydraulic transmission.[9] It was followed by a further six locomotives having Vulcan-Sinclair hydraulic couplings to mechanical gearboxes and two with dry clutches, all being in service by mid-1935.[10] Engines varied from 150 hp to 180 hp, which represented about the maximum for which mechanical transmissions had been developed in this country. Also tried was a Vulcan Foundry demonstration diesel-mechanical locomotive that was on loan during 1936.[11]

Despite the working party's earlier pronouncement concerning the cost of electric transmission, there were also two diesel-electric shunting locomotives of greater power than the diesel-mechanicals on trial in 1934. One was built by Armstrong Whitworth with a 250 hp Armstrong-Sulzer engine driving through a single, frame-mounted motor to a jackshaft. The other was produced by English Electric with a 300 hp engine driving two of the same firm's axle-hung motors, mechanical parts being made at the Forth Bank Works of Hawthorn, Leslie & Co. This locomotive, which was on extended loan during 1934 and 1935 before being taken into LMS stock, was also intended by its makers for general freight and local passenger train duties. It was capable of running at 35 mph and was fitted with both air and vacuum automatic braking systems.[12] In late 1934 it was tried on the Glasgow Underground between Glasgow Central and Bridgeton Cross in order to demonstrate that diesel traction was also a potential answer to reduction of smoke

Last of the three Leyland diesel-hydraulic four-wheeled railcars built in 1933 and officially taken into LMS stock in June 1934 was No. 29952. Their light weight and four-wheel layout reportedly gave the LMS cause for concern despite early favourable reports and reliability as well as riding qualities deteriorated. They ended their days at St. Rollox whence they were officially withdrawn in 1951.   COLLECTION R. J. ESSERY

The first of the LMS diesel shunters, No. 1831, was only used for a short time in its original guise and for its original purpose. It is seen here at Derby shed in September 1935. During 1940 it was converted to a mobile generating unit with the diesel engine directly coupled to an electrical generator, large radiator grilles installed at one end, hydraulic transmission and coupling rods removed and attached to a wagon carrying a container of heavy-duty electric cable.   W. POTTER

The first diesel locomotives to be built in quantity for any British railway company were the jackshaft-drive 0-6-0 shunters produced at Derby Works between May 1939 and June 1942. As with the subjects of this book, the diesel engine and electrical equipment were made by English Electric with overall design and manufacture of mechanical components by Derby. The jackshaft drive layout had inherent defects and they were succeeded by the 'twin motor' shunters, about which I hope to write in the not too distant future, that led directly to the widespread BR '08' Class. Forty were built with several being acquired by the War Department for home and overseas use. The last in BR service were withdrawn in 1967.   COLLECTION R. J. ESSERY

and fumes in the tunnels. Whilst this was partially successful, it left the problem of noxious diesel exhaust unresolved.

The hydraulic transmission on No. 1831 proved troublesome and it soon became a straight competition between mechanical and electrical drive for shunting locomotives.[13] By this time, a champion of electric transmission had arrived on the LMS in the form of C. E. Fairburn, who joined the company from English Electric in 1934 as Chief Electrical Engineer and was to become Deputy CME in 1937. Experience soon showed that there were only a few locations on the railway where 150–180 hp was sufficient to meet requirements and with Fairburn in a senior position in the company, there was in any case a bias developing towards the diesel-electric. He maintained that the previously-mentioned view of electrical transmission being more expensive than its mechanical counterpart was not true for the capacity and characteristics that trials with the various diesel shunters had shown to be necessary. Further requirements that Fairburn identified for an effective transmission system included the following:

- To endeavour as far as possible to use equipment that had already been established and tested out on the type of duty in question.
- To be able to accelerate and control the speed of the locomotive easily without losing the pull on the drawbar or changing it abruptly.
- The engine should be protected against transmission shocks due to unskilful driving or snatching of the train.
- The maximum power should be available over a large range of locomotive speeds.
- It should be possible to reverse the driving torque before the locomotive came to rest.

These requirements, he maintained, were best provided by electrical transmission. The result was that the LMS adopted the diesel-electric locomotive for its shunting task and for the remainder of its existence built no other type.[14] By the time Britain's railways were nationalised, the company was demonstrating savings with its diesel-electric shunters of 45% compared with steam locomotives.

In Germany, a lot of attention was drawn to the introduction of a high-speed, two-car streamlined diesel set called the *Fliegende Hamburger* running between Berlin and Hamburg. The LNER looked into the prospect of running the same kind of sets between King's Cross and Newcastle but in the event decided that the requisite speeds and loads were not possible and ended up producing the A4 Pacifics instead. The LMS took some of the features of the German train and together with application of lessons learned from their own various railcar and multiple unit trials produced a promising lightweight three-car, diesel-mechanical, articulated set driven by six 125 hp Leyland engines that was built at Derby Works in 1938. After trials, it entered regular service between St. Pancras and Nottingham but the war unfortunately put an end to its employment. Had war not intervened, it is quite likely that it would have been successful enough to be duplicated.

The pre-war LMS three-car articulated diesel-mechanical train is shown in this photograph. The three cars were numbered 80000-80002 and when built had valancing between the bogies but in July 1938, part way through initial trials, the valancing was removed as seen here. The train was advanced for its time with features such as air-powered, passenger-operable sliding doors under overall control of the guard and interlocked with the engine controls so that the train could not be started with a door open. The interior was steam heated from a boiler using exhaust gases from the outer cars.
COLLECTION R. J. ESSERY

With regard to heavy main-line operations, the need for economy was just as great. Conventional steam locomotives and their maintenance systems were being developed all the time with the goals of extending time and mileage between overhauls, reducing the time spent undergoing both overhauls and unscheduled repairs, and limiting the manpower requirement for preparation and disposal. Between the Grouping and Nationalisation, the LMS introduced such things as system-wide water treatment, taper boilers, roller bearings, rocking grates and hopper ashpans, manganese steel axlebox liners and a host of other details that were added to the list of improvements I referred to earlier. Another, more radical, approach was the construction and long-term trial of the turbine-driven No. 6202 that I described in *LMS Journal Nos. 10 and 11*. Despite all these efforts, however, the steam locomotive remained a labour-intensive machine in day-to-day service and such cherished goals as achieving 100,000 miles per year for Class 7 passenger engines eluded the locomotive engineers and operators. This was not just an eye-catching figure but represented a degree of cost-effectiveness significant to the overall economy of the railway. There were other drawbacks to the continued long-term use of steam locomotives, such as the provision and maintenance of vast and complex water supply and distribution systems as well as escalating costs of coal and the demands made by its distribution, storage and transfer into bunkers and tenders. In addition, the mechanised coal industry tended to produce smaller coal and 'fines' which were not very suitable for steam locomotives.

As previously mentioned, the development of airless fuel injection had enabled the advent of the lightweight, fast-running diesel engine, which opened up the possibilities for main-line diesel traction. In the late 1920s and early 1930s, chief progress in this field had been made in Denmark, Germany and Britain by such firms as Frichs, Krupp, Henschel, British Thomson-Houston and Armstrong-Whitworth supplying locomotives mainly to countries with coal supply problems in South America, the Middle East, Far East, and parts of the Soviet Union. Armstrong Whitworth also built an 800 hp main-line diesel-electric that was tried on the LNER in 1934. In America, the advance of diesel power was initially slow. After the advent of diesel shunters, or 'switchers', in 1924, little happened to further its cause until the first diesel-electric passenger locomotive was built by ALCO's Schenectady Works for the New York Central Railroad in 1929. For a time there wasn't much more progress but in 1934, the Burlington Railroad decided to try the new breed of engine and put into service its first main-line diesel locomotive. Its success was immediate and many other companies began to follow suit, slowly at first but with ever increasing enthusiasm.

No. 9 – MAIN LINE DIESEL-ELECTRICS Nos. 10000 and 10001

Sir Harold Hartley, Vice-President of the LMS, visited the United States in 1936 where he toured the newly-opened General Motors diesel plant at La Grange in Chicago and saw some of the early main-line diesels in action. He made a second visit in 1938, one of his principal aims being to ascertain how far the locomotives were giving satisfaction and how their operating costs compared with those of steam traction. By that time, there was a relatively large degree of experience, albeit still not huge, with main-line diesel traction across the Atlantic and Sir Harold was able to reach a firm conclusion. After returning to England in June 1938 he stated, 'There is little doubt that under American operating conditions the diesel locomotive has come to stay and as the cost of manufacture diminishes, its range of usefulness will be extended. In this country, however, the operating conditions are so different that it may be difficult to find conditions under which the diesel locomotive at its present cost offers advantages over the modern steam locomotive'. At that time, estimated first cost of a main-line diesel-electric was four to five times that of an equivalent steam locomotive and for that to be justified, considerable increases in availability and daily mileage had to be achieved. In Sir Harold's opinion, this wasn't possible on the LMS of 1938.

The second world war exacerbated the problems of operating steam locomotives, with the quality of coal decreasing markedly as well as its cost continuing to soar, and thoughts were turning to the steps that would have to be taken to improve matters. Three types of motive power that could answer at least some of the main-line problems confronting Britain's postwar railways were electric, gas turbine and diesel. All promised greater availability, reduced manpower requirements and more congenial working conditions. The latter was a major consideration for recruitment and retention of staff in a climate of virtually full postwar employment and the growing expectation among skilled and semi-skilled workers of an improved working environment. Electric, gas turbine and diesel locomotives would also have some of the benefits identified for 'Turbomotive' in 1932, i.e., no hammer blow, even drawbar pull, greater starting tractive effort and increased mechanical efficiency. Indeed, the starting tractive effort for these alternative power forms could be even greater because a larger proportion of the total locomotive weight, possibly all of it, would rest on driven wheels. Acceleration should also be better because the total power output would be available throughout the whole speed range, limited to some extent by adhesion and characteristics of the transmission, whereas a conventional steam locomotive could not use as much steam as the boiler could supply until a critical speed was reached at which the cylinders could effectively utilise the full output. The resultant saving in time could have a marked effect on timetables over busy routes[15].

The main drawback to all the alternatives was cost of both initial purchase and maintenance. In the case of electrification, the outlay on fixed equipment before a single train could run was enormous and in austerity-era Britain money was tight. A few gas turbine or diesel locomotives, though, could be built at a much lower cost for extended trials. The spread of main-line diesel traction in America had continued to gather pace. East of Chicago, where there was ready access to coal mines and much of the freight traffic emanated from them, it was relatively slow but to the west, where coal was difficult to obtain and oil firing common, it was rapid. The Santa Fé Railroad bought its last steam locomotive in 1942 and by the end of the second world war, 75% of new locomotive orders throughout the USA were for diesels. The experience of main-line diesel traction was therefore commensurately greater than it had been in 1938 and by 1946 what were seen as meaningful statistics had been produced showing its cost-effectiveness.

Despite much higher initial unit costs and the need to establish fuelling and maintenance facilities, the new motive power made economic sense providing it ran high mileages. The Pennsylvania Railroad, for instance, showed in 1946 that its diesel-hauled passenger trains ran for a little under 80% of the cost per mile of its steam-hauled services and freight cost per mile was just over 80%, both results taking into account fuel, maintenance and labour. Consequently, it had shelved plans to extend its electrified route from Harrisburg to Pittsburgh and Cincinatti in the expectation that diesel traction would satisfy its needs more economically. These figures were thought by some British and Canadian engineers to be somewhat dubious but detailed and well-documented tests undertaken by the New York Central the same year between Harmon and Chicago demonstrated clear savings. Six of the modern 'Niagara' Class 4-8-4 steam engines were rostered to haul passenger trains over the 928 mile route alongside twin-unit 4,000 hp diesel-electrics. Average mileage per day in service achieved in the year by the 'Niagaras' was 862 whereas the diesels averaged 904. Annual mileage and availability figures were 288,000 and 69% for steam against 324,000 and 74.2% for diesel. Although total operating costs for NYC diesels were 99% of those for steam locomotives, this greater availability and mileage resulted in an overall 9% saving per mile by diesels when all costs were included. Such mileages were unheard of and considered probably to be unattainable in Britain because of the wholly different nature of the railways and their operating conditions but the principles were held to apply.

It seemed to some people in the immediate post-war LMS, therefore, that diesels quite possibly represented the way forward even though Roland Bond and some other senior officers of the company were still looking to steam turbine propulsion for express passenger work. Fairburn had become acting CME in 1942 followed by his appointment as CME in 1944 and it would be natural to think that he would be in favour of main-line diesel-electrics. In his opinion, however, Sir Harold Hartley's conclusion of 1938 that the enormous first cost could not be justified under British operating conditions still applied. Fairburn's Principal Assistant, H. G. Ivatt, took a somewhat different view, convinced that the potential of main-line diesel traction should be investigated practically, and in a memo dated 25th January 1945 he urged the production of what was described as a B-C-B, or 4-6-4, main-line locomotive with electric transmission. In the same year, several other schemes were sketched out by Derby Locomotive Drawing Office at Ivatt's instigation for 1,600 hp diesel-electrics powered by English Electric 16SVT engines and using electrical equipment the same or closely similar to that being used in the erection of locomotives at Dick, Kerr Works for the Egyptian Railways. One, to drawing DD-3784, was for an A1A-A1A whilst DD-3794 showed a 1A-Bo-A1, both schemes having the same internal layout and body with plain ends and no bonnets. Each would have had four traction motors, been 52ft 8in long over the buffers, 9ft wide, 12ft 10½in high and weighed about 110 tons. I have also seen it reported that a Do-Do version was sketched with eight traction motors,

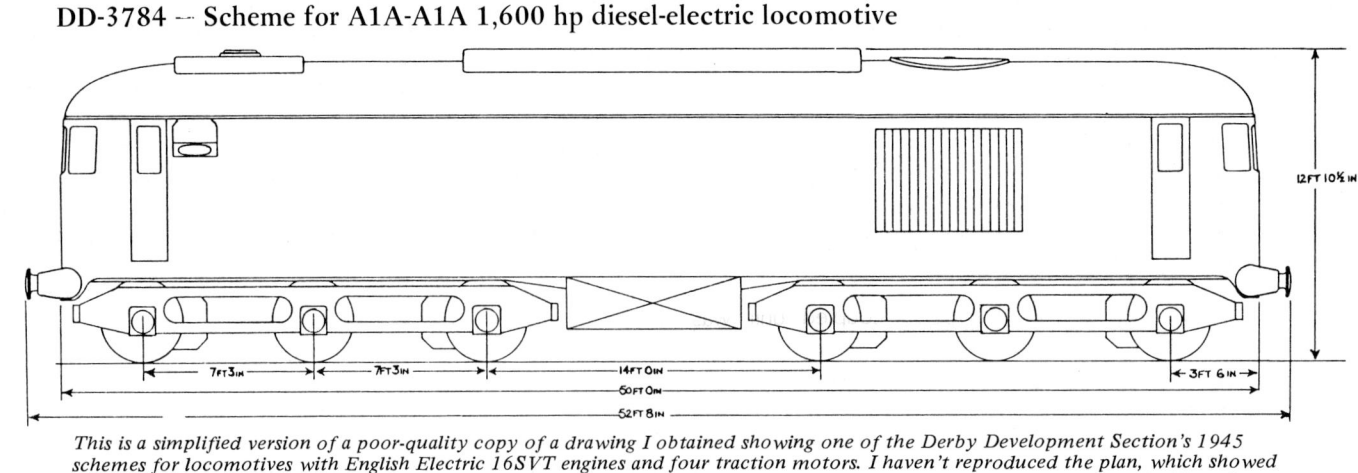

DD-3784 — Scheme for A1A-A1A 1,600 hp diesel-electric locomotive

This is a simplified version of a poor-quality copy of a drawing I obtained showing one of the Derby Development Section's 1945 schemes for locomotives with English Electric 16SVT engines and four traction motors. I haven't reproduced the plan, which showed that since there was no nose section, the traction motor ventilation blowers would have been mounted above each bogie. The other large components mounted in the nose pieces of the eventual design — the air compressors — were to have been below the engine and the boiler would have been mounted on the locomotive centreline with water tanks on either side. Water capacity was to have been 550 gallons. Apart from the dimensions indicated on the drawing here, overall width was given as 9ft 0in.

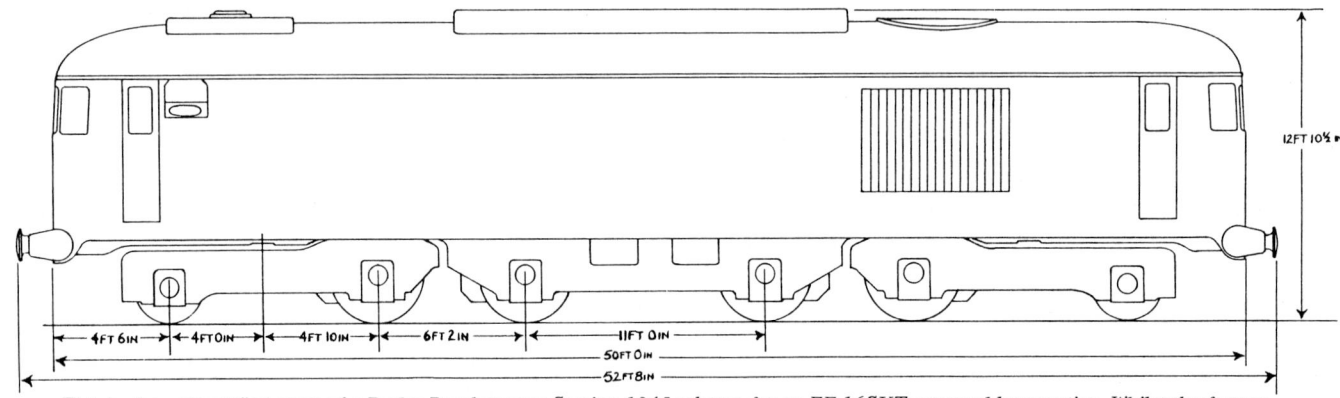

DD-3794 — Scheme for 1A-Bo-A1 1,600 hp diesel-electric locomotive

This is also a simplified copy of a Derby Development Section 1945 scheme for an EE 16SVT-powered locomotive. Whilst the frames and bogies were quite different from DD3784, the body shell and its internal layout were the same. Once again, four traction motors were to have been used — two on the middle axles fitted into the main frames and one on the inner axle of each bogie. Driven wheels would have been 4ft 0in diameter and carrying wheels 3ft 0in.

3ft 0in wheels and a 5ft 10in + 7ft 10in + 5ft 10in wheelbase to each bogie but I haven't been able to find any trace of the drawing[16]. The locomotive apparently was to be 61ft 2in over buffers with bogie centres at 33ft 0in and weigh 130 tons. These schemes, however, didn't attract a great deal of enthusiasm from Fairburn and the only progress towards main-line diesel traction was a discussion he had with British Thomson-Houston just before his death in October 1945 about the possibility of a Paxman-engined 1,500 hp locomotive capable of undertaking the duties allocated to 2-6-4 tank engines.

Fairburn's successor, H. G. Ivatt, was appointed CME in January 1946 and promptly began seeking support for the 1,600 hp proposal as well as for an 800 hp machine to be used on secondary services. He had the idea that operation of main-line diesels in Britain would act as a showcase for the firms producing the engines and transmissions, which would lead to overseas orders. Consequently, it would be reasonable to ask them to contribute to the first cost of producing some experimental machines, particularly if the equipment used was of standard, off-the-shelf, design. During a visit to Derby by the Company President, Sir William Wood, in December 1945, Ivatt outlined his scheme and Sir William granted permission for negotiations to be opened with appropriate manufacturers. Ivatt lost no time and immediately began talks with BTH and Crompton-Parkinson as well as English Electric concerning both 1,600 and 800 hp proposals but subsequently decided that he would restrict negotiations to one company for each in the interests of expediency. First priority was the 1,600 hp scheme and, possibly because of existing contacts to do with the 350 hp shunters that were being built, as well as the fact that twelve-month exchanges of Works personnel were being undertaken between the two companies, he chose English Electric[17]. It is also, of course, significant that the 1945 proposals had been drawn round English Electric 16SVT engines.

On 20th May 1946, a meeting took place between representatives of the LMS and the English Electric Company, at which tentative agreement was reached concerning the building of what was described as, 'A trial diesel-electric locomotive of 3,200 hp in the form of two bogie-mounted units each of 1,600 hp coupled together'. The units were to be capable of working singly, in which case each one would be the equivalent of a Class 5

No. 9 — MAIN LINE DIESEL-ELECTRICS Nos. 10000 and 10001

mixed traffic engine, or in multiple when they would be capable of taking Class 7 loads with only a single crew. The agreement stated, 'The English Electric Company to provide the diesel engine and electrical equipment at their own expense. The LMS to design and construct the chassis portion consisting of bogies, frames, cabs etc. After the locomotive has demonstrated its performance on the road for a sufficient period, the LMS have the option of taking over the locomotive at an agreed value or the English Electric Company to pay the LMS for the making of parts and take over the locomotive themselves.' The demonstration of performance was to include operating in multiple on the 'Royal Scot' non-stop from London to Glasgow for a week.

On 29th May, Ivatt placed before the Traffic Committee his recommendation that negotiations were continued and a firm agreement reached. This recommendation was endorsed by the Committee in Minute 7673A, which ended, 'Approved so far as the Mechanical and Electrical Engineering Committee is concerned', and authorisation for construction was duly granted under NWO 6905. Something that was sadly wrong was the estimated cost to the LMS of the project, the minute recording that, 'On a preliminary estimate (the cost) was not expected to exceed £15,000'. As it turned out, this was about a fifth of the final outlay for the two units that had to be met by the LMS and BR.

A technical paper was produced by the CME's Department in September 1946 supporting the decision to build the locomotives, stating that the expected thermal efficiency was three times that of a steam locomotive and one and a half times that of an electric whilst they would be, 'Made up of many light, renewable parts which can be serviced or replaced during the turn-round times between rostered hours of duty'. The possible advantages of the locomotives were identified as:

1. Greater availability due to quick turn-round times and sectionalised maintenance. In spite of high first cost, the cost per mile with high availability may still be lower.
2. Improved schedules and timekeeping due to more rapid acceleration.
3. Absence of smoke and dirt.

The way in which these advantages were stated seems to me significant. The cost per mile is only mentioned at the end of the first paragraph and it was only estimated that it *may* have proved to be lower. In other words, it was perhaps no longer either the overriding consideration in trying main-line diesel traction or a bar to its eventual adoption should major savings not be achieved.

The description of a single 3,200 hp locomotive that could be split into two was commonly used whilst 10000 and 10001 were being designed. Once the first of them entered traffic, however, they were generally referred to as two locomotives that could work together. The coupled unit was to be compared on Anglo-Scottish services against the two improved Stanier Pacifics, Nos. 6256 and 6257, as well as the separate entities being tried out on intermediate and mixed traffic services.[18] The routes envisaged for the individual units included London suburban passenger services to Bletchley and Luton, passenger and freight workings on the North Stafford section round Stoke, and in the Derby, Nottingham and Leicester areas. Power requirements for the Euston–Glasgow trains were calculated to be as shown in the table.

SHP required – Euston to Glasgow. Load 552 tons to Crewe then 482 tons.

Section	Sustained SHP	Maximum SHP
Euston – Tring	1,590	1,750 for 4 minutes
Tring – Rugby	1,590	1,750 for 6 minutes
Rugby – Stafford	1,590	1,720 for 3 minutes
		1,840 for 4 minutes
Stafford – Crewe	1,590	1,770 for 6 minutes
Crewe – Carnforth	1,670	2,170 for 3 minutes
		1,840 for 15 minutes
		1,920 for 4 minutes
Carnforth – Shap Summit	1,590	1,970 for 18 minutes
Shap Summit – Carlisle	500	1,085 for 14 minutes
Carlisle – Beattock Station	1,890	2,090 for 6 minutes
		2,260 for 7 minutes
Beattock Station – Beattock Summit	1,790	1,990 for 6 minutes
Beattock Summit – Glasgow	670	1,590 for 4 minutes
		1,340 for 5 minutes
		1,250 for 7 minutes

Four months later it was decided that negotiations for construction of an 800 hp Bo-Bo 'of comparable capacity to the Company's small 2-6-2 tank locomotives' would be opened with British Thomson-Houston along the same lines as the agreement reached with English Electric. This locomotive, No. 10800, was eventually built by the North British Locomotive Co. with a Paxman engine and BTH electrical gear in 1950. The final proposal with which the LMS was concerned was for the Fell diesel-mechanical locomotive, the Board approving an agreement in October 1947 with Davey, Paxman & Co., Shell Refining & Marketing Co., and Lt. Col. L. F. R. Fell for a 4-8-4 similar in capacity to one unit of the 3,200 hp diesel-electric already ordered and to be tried out in competition with it. The agreement was similar to those already described, the locomotive to be built at Derby Works with the contractors providing the engines, transmission and control gear at their own expense pending successful performance. In the event, the locomotive was 2,000 hp but it wasn't put into traffic until 1951.

Whilst all this activity had been going on, the LMS was also showing interest in gas turbine traction. Studies and some initial experiments were being carried out in America with gas turbines for rail locomotives running on pulverised coal. F. C. Johanssen of the LMS Scientific Research Department maintained contact with some of the people closely involved in the project but nothing particularly promising arose from it.[19] Encouraged from without by Sir William Stanier, Ivatt was also showing a keen interest in the development of oil-fuelled gas turbines, which were becoming well-established in the aviation industry, and saw them as potential rivals to diesel engines. At his instigation, a report was prepared in March 1946 by two of the CME's assistants, E. S. Cox and F. A. Harper, which identified three potential advantages of gas turbines over diesels. They were reduced first costs and maintenance costs, lighter weight for a given power, and cheaper fuel, even though fuel consumption was foreseen as higher than that of a diesel engine. T. M. Herbert, head of the Derby Research Department, arranged for Cox and Johanssen to keep a close eye on progress in the gas turbine field, to compare notes and information, and to prepare reports from time to time. Cox and Harper visited Power Jets Ltd. at Leicester to discuss possible locomotive applications in March 1946 and Harper went to Brown Boverei in Switzerland in July. Harper's visit followed an unsolicited approach from the Swiss company with particulars of a gas turbine locomotive they had built for the Swiss Federal Railways that was being tested in France.

Accordingly, Ivatt reported to the M&EE Committee in April 1946 that he, 'Proposed to have provision made in the Company's diesel-electric designs whereby it would be possible to substitute a gas turbine for the diesel unit'. Outline drawings showing dimensions, weights, etc. were supplied to Brown Boverei and BTH. One of Cox and Johanssen's progress reports in January 1947 indicated that contact was being maintained with BTH over a proposed power plant of 2,000 hp consisting of an axial flow compressor driven by a high-pressure turbine running at 5,500 rpm and a free low-pressure turbine directly driving the electrical generator. It was claimed that the two-turbine arrangement would give better efficiency at partial loads. The report concluded, 'The design is still in the preliminary stages but the possibility of installing the unit in the chassis of the 1,600 hp LMS diesel-electric loco is being kept in mind'. During the same month, representatives of Brown Boverei visited Derby to talk about the supply of a proposed 2,500 hp unit with an auxiliary diesel engine for starting and manoeuvring at low speed, which would be similar to the GWR gas turbine design.

In the event, the LMS decided not to pursue the gas turbine option, as development was slow and performance much more of an unknown quantity than that of diesel-electrics. The company's final position on alternative forms of traction was stated in a report entitled 'LMS Railway Power Plant' prepared in the latter part of 1947, which read, 'The LMS feels that the conventional reciprocating steam locomotive is still capable of considerable advance and that the ceiling of operating availability and maintenance cost per mile has not yet been reached. If any departure from the simple, cheap, rugged and reliable steam locomotive of normal aspect is envisaged for the sake of higher thermal efficiency or still higher availability, then this Company believes that a complete break away from steam towards diesel traction is the logical step to take.' Since Nationalisation was then a fact waiting to happen, this would appear to be the LMS message to its successors. By that time, of course, construction of No. 10000 was under way and Derby Works was going to make sure it was completed as an LMS locomotive.[20]

In October 1946, this artist's impression of No. 10000 was issued and appeared in Locomotives of the LMS. *The two most obvious differences from what was actually built are the shape of the nose compartments, with raised centres and deep side windows, and the carriage-style windows in the body sides. No engine compartment doors are depicted and the bogies are the symmetrical ones with two traction motors each that were designed before English Electric decided that three motors were needed.*

No. 9 – MAIN LINE DIESEL-ELECTRICS Nos. 10000 and 10001

CONSTRUCTION AND MODIFICATIONS

This official LMS photograph was taken when 10000 was first completed and shows it resplendent in black and silver livery with its 'LMS' body side lettering.
BRITISH RAILWAYS LMR, CTY. J. JENNISON

Unlike previous LMS locomotive classes, introduction of the 1,600 hp diesel-electrics was surrounded by a glare of publicity from the commencement of their design and throughout construction. It was confidently stated that the weight of the (combined) locomotive would be 220 tons and it would be capable of 100 mph. There was even an artist's impression issued in October 1946 of No. 10000 on its own as well as one of the two units working in multiple, both of which were slightly incorrect in the cab/nose area and body sides. This advance publicity would seem to have been a risky move on the part of the LMS, as when Derby Works and English Electric began serious work on the project they had less than eighteen months in which to finish it before Nationalisation. That they did so with a little time to spare in the austerity days when materials were often difficult to obtain is the highest possible credit to all concerned, particularly in view of the design's subsequent success. The importance that English Electric attached to the project is indicated by the fact that they diverted engines, generators and traction motors to it from their Egyptian state railways order and had to make up the shortfall later.

The production of locomotives as a joint venture with construction effort taking place at several sites was something for which the LMS had little experience and great care had to be taken to ensure that timescales were met for individual items. The contract for supply of components from English Electric was dated 29th November 1946 and on 8th March 1947 a document was issued that laid out the agreed division of work between the companies. It is interesting to note that the English Electric schedule of apparatus refers to the contract as being for a development locomotive. Derby Locomotive Drawing Office completed the design in April and work on the main frames began on 10th July. The construction schedule agreed was as follows:

July	10th	-	Start main frames.
	15th	-	Electrical equipment begins to arrive from EE.
	31st	-	Body sides available.
August	22nd	-	Main frames complete.
	31st	-	Axles ready for motors.
September	20th	-	Master controller, equipment frames, radiator panels, radiator fan and exhausters delivered.
	29th	-	Control equipment in place and cabs ready. Power unit and radiators delivered.
October	2nd	-	Wired.
	8th	-	Frames fitted out.
	10th	-	Gear wheels ready for pressing onto axles.
	13th	-	Engine, radiator fan and motor fitted.
	27th	-	Traction motors, gear cases and batteries delivered.
November	21st	-	Wheeled.
	22nd	-	Body completed for cabs to be fitted and primer applied.
	25th	-	Steam heat boiler installed.
December	1st	-	Painted.
	4th	-	Started.

As Mechanical Engineer (Locomotive Works), Roland Bond was given the job of chairing meetings to co-ordinate design, supply of materials and power equipment from the contractors as well as production in the Derby Works shops. There was much to be learned about building the underframe, body and fabricated bogies but the Works Manager, Eric Robson, had been trained in carriage and wagon work and, with wide experience of building all-steel coaching stock, he was able to guide the men in the shops through many difficult production problems. In particular, he worked closely with the foreman of the diesel shop who at the time was Bert Barlow.

The wheel arrangement was originally to have been A1A-A1A, as first suggested on DD-3784, and bogie design was virtually completed for that layout. At a late stage, however, English Electric advised that they wanted all axles powered and the design was altered to Co-Co with uneven axle spacing.

The construction schedule was met to within a few days. No. 10000 left No. 10A diesel shop on 5th December and emerged from the paint shop under her own power three days later with H. G. Ivatt at the controls. There was a last-minute panic when the locomotive was tested the evening before the official roll-out and the two bogies tried to set off in opposite directions! A supply of midnight oil was ordered and some rewiring of the control cubicle cured the problem but there was one small drama still to go. During the final spit and polish session prior to roll-out, someone left a handful of cotton waste on top of the exhaust and when Ivatt started the engine it caught fire and fell onto the floor. Fortunately, it was quickly extinguished by one of the apprentices who was standing by and apart from some evil-smelling smoke drifting over the assembled crowd, all was well.

After clearance tests on the 4½ chain curve at Trent, 10000 officially entered traffic on 13th December. Construction of 10001 was delayed because of the need to concentrate on steam locomotive building and repair at Derby Works for a time after everything had been subjugated to getting 10000 finished. Consequently, the second locomotive didn't appear until nearly seven months later, officially entering traffic on 5th July 1948. Once both locomotives were in service, they became known among enthusiasts as 'the twins' although the term was never used officially and was frowned on by senior BR men. As will be seen later, although referred to as twins, the locomotives were never identical in all details.

The two locomotives were built as Lot No. 198 to Order No. 2510, which was issued in May 1947. Since 10001 was completed seven months after 10000, there were a couple of detail differences incorporated in the light of experience, which will be described later. Construction cost was estimated at £78,566 per locomotive, of which £40,700 would be met by English Electric and £37,866 by the LMS. The two together would therefore be £156,331 which, considering that improved Pacifics were being built for less than £23,000 each, was an absolutely enormous amount to pay. It is also significant that the amount to be met by the Railway was five times greater than had been estimated when M&EE Committee approval had been given, which is an indication of the importance attached to the project. Actual cost as recorded on the engine history cards was £300 less for 10000 and £301 less for 10001.

Nomenclature for which end of the locomotive was which varied. The end nearest to the radiator louvres was variously called the front, No. 1 end, or south end; the other was the rear, hind end, No. 2 end, or north end. The right-hand side when looking towards the No. 1 end was referred to at Derby Works as the west side and the left as the east. The compass points were simply the orientation of the locomotives when they were built in the diesel shop. This apparently had at least one repercussion when an electrician who was later called out to a problem on No. 10000 found on taking his first look inside the electrical cupboard that all the wires at the No. 2 end had tags with 'N' on them. This was for orientation during installation but the poor man, not knowing it, thought for a time that all the wires were negative! It became the norm to refer to the sides of the locomotive as left or right when looking towards the No. 1 end, which is the convention I will use in this book.

Leading particulars were as follows:

Overall length	61ft 2in
Overall width	9ft 3in
Notional overall height	12ft 11 5⁄16in
Total wheelbase	51ft 2in total
Bogie wheelbase	8ft + 7ft 8in
Bogie centres	35ft 6in
Wheel diameter	3ft 6in
Tractive effort	Maximum possible starting 41,400 lb
	Maximum for one hour 18,500 lb @ 26 mph
	Maximum continuous 15,000 lb @ 32 mph
Rail hp at continuous rating	1,295
Maximum speed	93 mph
Minimum curve radius	4½ chains dead slow
Weight empty	122 tons 9 cwt
Weight in working order	127 tons 13 cwt

Both were initially allocated to Engine Diagram 279. Later alterations to the train heating system increased the weight in working order to 130 tons 14 cwt and ED 279A was issued to reflect this. Power classification was originally 5P 5F but when the locomotives went to the Southern Region in 1953 it became 6P 5F. On their return to the LMR in 1955 it reverted to 5P 5F and by withdrawal it was simply 5.[21] Their official BR modernisation scheme power range was Type 3 and class designation was Class 34 but this seems rarely, if ever, to have been used and there was nothing on the locomotives to indicate it. When the Eastern Region introduced its own classification, they were annotated D16/1.

The description of each locomotive as being 1,600 hp was a little misleading. Although this was the maximum installed power that the engine produced, the maximum rating of the traction motors only added up to 1,200 hp, the remaining 400hp being used to overcome system losses and to drive the auxiliary generator as will be described later.

ENGINE

The English Electric 16SVT Mk. 1, which was developed and made at the Willans & Robinson Works in Rugby, was a four stroke, 16-cylinder, turbocharged V16 of about 15,080 cu in (247 litres) displace-

The English Electric 16SVT Mk 1 diesel engine with EE823A main generator and EE909 auxiliary generator is shown in this illustration. The generators are seen at the left-hand side of the picture whilst at either end of the cylinder banks are the Brown-Boverei turbochargers. The two water pumps and oil pumps can be seen at the right-hand end of the crankcase.
ENGLISH ELECTRIC CO., CTY. J. JENNISON

No. 9 – MAIN LINE DIESEL-ELECTRICS Nos. 10000 and 10001

ment running at a maximum of 750 rpm.[22] It was a direct descendant of the 'K' series engines, the first of which was used in the 300 hp shunter demonstrated on the LMS in 1934 and purchased in 1936. That had been a normally aspirated, straight six unit developing 50 hp per cylinder but subsequent development had resulted in over 100 hp per cylinder being obtainable from a turbocharged V16. The engine had main and auxiliary generators attached at the rear so that they formed a single unit mounted on main frame cross stretchers. There were three primary mounts with rubber intermediate pads and two auxiliary spring mountings under the main generator, the design of the mounts ensuring that the engine would be independent of any flexing of the locomotive frame and so avoid strain on the crankshaft. The two cylinder banks were labelled A and B, the former being on the left-hand side of the locomotive.

Cylinder block and crankcase were made from two iron castings split along the centreline and reinforced by a cast-steel bed plate incorporating the sump, flywheel housing and generator mounting. A one-piece carbon steel crankshaft with a vibration damper at the free end ran in nine whitemetal bearings with steel shells, every one of the eight cranks being driven by a forged alloy-steel connecting rod from each cylinder bank. Big end bearings were bronze shells lined with white metal and small ends were phosphor-bronze. Cylinder liners were cast-iron and the cast-aluminium alloy pistons had combustion chambers formed in the crowns as well as three compression rings and two scraper rings. Each cylinder bank had its own built-up camshaft in a tunnel cast into the crankcase, driven by triple chains from spur gears at the rear of the crankshaft. Removable cams were fitted to the camshafts and roller cam followers drove the inlet valves, exhaust valves, and fuel injection pumps in each individual, cast-iron cylinder head. Injection pumps on 10000 were made by Bryce Berger whilst the injectors were by CAV.

Although maximum engine power output available at 750 rpm was 1,760 hp, it was set on the LMS locomotives at 1,600 hp, which was controlled by a governor driven from one of the camshafts at the flywheel end. A servo piston operated by the lubricating oil system moved racks along the line of injectors for each cylinder bank. Teeth on the racks engaged gears on

Engine cooling system schematic

This English Electric schematic diagram was kindly provided by Alstom Transport Services and shows the cooling system for the 16sVT engine.

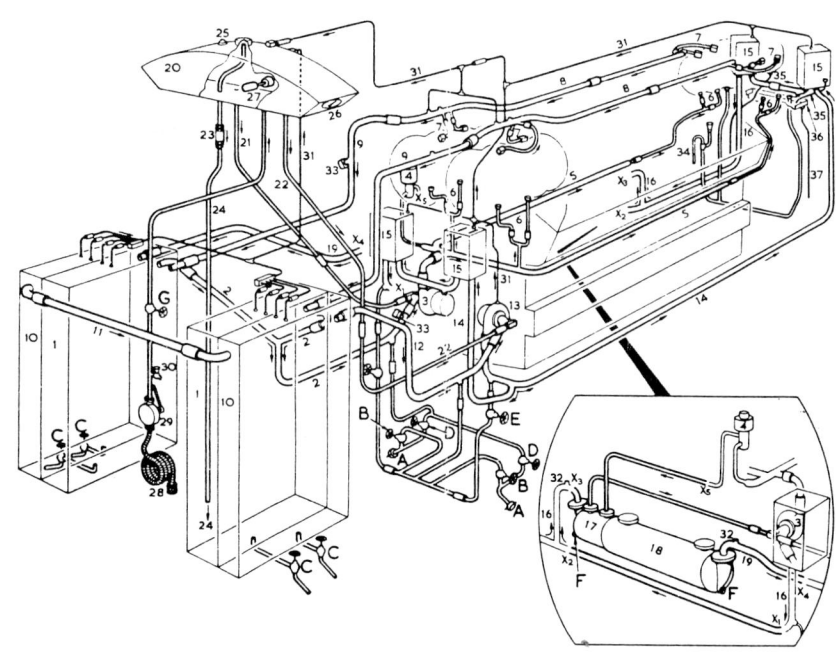

COOLING WATER SYSTEM

ENGINE COOLING SYSTEM
1. RADIATOR (INNER)
2. OUTLET PIPES TO PUMP
3. JACKET COOLING WATER PUMP
4. THERMOSTATIC DIVERSION VALVE (air-operated)
5. INLET RAIL TO CYLINDER JACKETS
6. INLETS TO TURBO-BLOWER
7. OUTLETS FROM TURBO-BLOWER
8. OUTLET MANIFOLD FROM CYLINDER HEADS
9. RETURN PIPE TO RADIATOR

CHARGECOOLER AND LUB. OIL COOLER SYSTEM
10. RADIATOR (OUTER)
11. RADIATORS TRANSFER PIPE
12. OUTLET PIPE TO PUMP
13. CHARGECOOLERS AND LUB. OIL COOLER COOLING WATER PUMP
14. PIPE, PUMP TO CHARGECOOLER
15. CHARGECOOLER
16. PIPE, CHARGECOOLERS TO LUB. OIL COOLER
17. CHARGECOOLER WATER HEATER (from jacket water)
18. LUB. OIL COOLER
19. PIPE, LUB. OIL COOLER TO R.H. RADIATOR

HEADER TANK
20. HEADER TANK FOR BOTH SYSTEMS
21. MAKE-UP PIPE FOR ENGINE COOLING SYSTEM
22. MAKE-UP PIPE FOR CHARGECOOLERS AND LUB. OIL COOLER SYSTEM
23. PRESSURISING VALVE
24. OVERFLOW PIPE
25. ANTI-VACUUM VALVE
26. CONTENTS GAUGE (each side of tank)
27. LOW-LEVEL SHUT-DOWN SWITCH
28. FLEXIBLE SUCTION HOSE WITH STRAINER
29. EMERGENCY-FILLING HAND PUMP
30. PRIMING COCK

31. VENT PIPES TO HEADER TANK
32. THERMOMETER POCKET
33. TEMPERATURE PROBE FOR RADIATOR SHUTTER CONTROL
34. TURBO-BLOWER CASING DRAIN AND WATER SEAL (each end of engine)
35. CHARGECOOLER CONDENSATE DRAIN
36. DRIP TRAY
37. DRIP TRAY DRAIN

DRAINING AND REFILLING POINTS
A. DRAINING AND REFILLING CONNECTION (each side of loco.)
B. DRAINING AND REFILLING VALVE (each side of loco.)
C. RADIATOR DRAIN VALVE
D. ENGINE COOLING SYSTEM DRAIN VALVE
E. CHARGECOOLERS AND LUB. OIL COOLERS SYSTEM DRAIN VALVE
F. LUB. OIL COOLER DRAIN PLUG
G. EMERGENCY-FILLING HAND PUMP VALVE

Engine lubrication system schematic

This diagram was also provided by Alstom Transport Services and illustrates the English Electric 16SVT engine lubrication system.

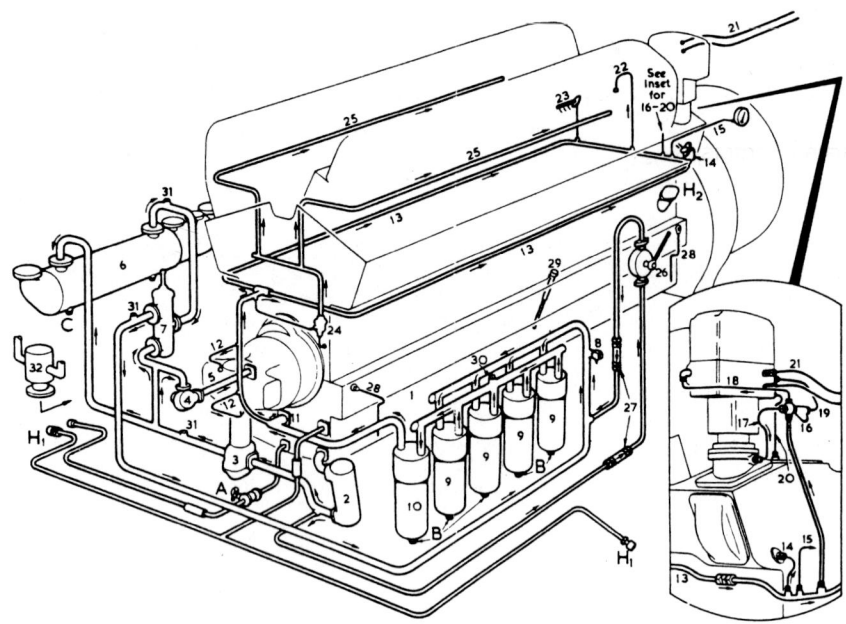

LUB. OIL SYSTEM

1. BEDPLATE SUMP
2. SUCTION STRAINER
3. ENGINE-DRIVEN PUMP
4. H.P. RELIEF VALVE
5. H.P. RELIEF PIPE TO BEDPLATE SUMP
6. LUB. OIL COOLER
7. THERMOSTATIC VALVE
8. SAMPLING VALVE
9. FILTER
10. STRAINER
11. INLET TO MAIN SYSTEM
12. H.P. OIL TO AUXILIARY DRIVE
13. H.P. OIL TO CAMSHAFT BEARINGS
14. H.P. OIL TO 'B' BANK CAMSHAFT DRIVE CHAIN SPRAYER
15. H.P. OIL TO PRESSURE GAUGE
16. STRAINER
17. H.P. OIL TO GOVERNOR DRIVE
18. H.P. OIL TO GOVERNOR L.O. & SHUT-DOWN DEVICE
19. H.P. OIL TO GOVERNOR (for vane motor operation)
20. DRAIN TO CRANKCASE
21. OIL TO AND FROM VANE MOTOR
22. H.P. OIL TO CAMSHAFT DRIVE CHAIN TENSIONER
23. H.P. OIL TO 'A' BANK CAMSHAFT DRIVE CHAIN SPRAYER
24. PRESSURE REDUCING VALVE
25. L.P. OIL TO VALVE GEAR
26. HAND PRIMING PUMP
27. NON-RETURN VALVES
28. BEDPLATE VALANCE DRAINS (each end, each side)
29. OIL LEVEL DIPSTICK (on 'A' bank side of engine)
30. AIR VENT PLUG
31. THERMOMETER POCKET
32. CRANKCASE BREATHER (on chargecoolers bracket on auxiliary drive casing)

DRAINING AND REFILLING POINTS

A. BEDPLATE SUMP DRAIN VALVE (padlocked)
B. FILTERS AND STRAINER DRAIN COCKS
C. LUB. OIL COOLER DRAIN COCK (each end of cylinder)
H₁. PRESSURE FILLER (each side of loco.)
H₂. HAND FILLER ON CRANKCASE DOOR (on 'A' bank side of engine)

---

each pump that rotated an internal helix and changed the amount of fuel delivered to the cylinders. Manual adjustment of maximum output with the governor in its neutral position was possible by moving the racks – drawing them out increased the fuel supply.

The exhaust manifolds were in the vee between the cylinders and from them the exhaust gases were directed to drive four Brown Boverei turbochargers, each having its own lubrication system and supplying four cylinders with air drawn in through louvres in the body sides via Vokes filters. From the turbochargers, the exhaust was taken to outlets in the roof above the end of the engine compartment.

The engine was water cooled, total capacity of the system being 193 gallons, of which 40 gallons was contained in two Serck side radiators and their associated header tanks just behind the bogie centreline at the No. I end. Water was circulated through galleries in the block by two pumps, one for each cylinder bank, mounted at the front of the engine and driven by spur gears on the free end of the crankshaft. Cooling air was drawn in via double columns of louvres in the body sides, through the radiators, and then exhausted through a large circular opening in the roof by an EE728/1A motor-driven fan, which was protected by a circular mesh panel. Fan speed and the opening angle of the louvres were automatically controlled by thermostats in order to maintain an optimum coolant temperature.

Lubrication was from a 160 gallon sump in the engine bed. There were two mechanical, engine-driven pumps. One drew oil from the sump into oil coolers built in to the side radiators and the second took it from the coolers and through filters whence it was fed under pressure through galleries in the crankcase, crankshaft, and cylinder blocks to the main crankshaft journals, big end journals, camshaft bearings and drive, pump drives, and governor. Galleries in the connecting rods carried oil from the big end bearings up to the small ends, gudgeon pins and pistons. A reducing valve fed oil to a lower pressure system that took it to the valves whilst the cams and rollers were splash lubricated by oil draining into wells in the camshaft tunnels.

FUEL SYSTEM

Eight hundred and fifteen gallons of fuel was carried in two main tanks that were positioned either side of the walkway

No. 9 — MAIN LINE DIESEL-ELECTRICS Nos. 10000 and 10001

through the locomotive with a balance pipe between them and an 85 gallon service tank above them. Fillers were provided behind a drop-down flap below the radiator louvres for pressure refuelling and also at the top so that, in an emergency, hand refuelling could be used. A primary pump, driven from the same point as the water pumps, transferred oil from the main tank up to the service tank whence it was gravity fed to the injector pumps. There was also a semi-rotary hand pump that was used to ensure the service tank was full before starting and could be employed to top up the service tank if the primary pump failed. A full service tank was sufficient for between about 75 and 110 miles running, depending on the load.

With full main and service tanks, unrefuelled range was just over 1,000 miles at average consumption but if the fuel level was allowed to get too low, cavitation could occur, resulting in air entering the fuel lines, which would cause rough running and loss of power. For some reason, this was particularly problematic when the locomotives were on the Southern Region and instructions were issued there to keep the fuel contents above half. Whether this was because of the increased power output at which the engines were made to operate during their stay at Nine Elms, which is described later, I don't know.

GENERATORS AND TRACTION MOTORS

The main generator was an English Electric EE 823A type DC unit and like much of the electrical gear, including the auxiliary generator, traction motors, other electric motors and control gear, was made at the Phoenix Works in Bradford. It had 8 poles, two separate windings and a continuous rating of 1,080 kW at 650 volts and 1,660 amps. The generator body register was bolted to an extension of the engine bedplate at the flywheel end. It had a single, sealed and grease-packed bearing, was driven directly from the engine crankshaft, and was self-ventilating, i.e., there was no forced ventilation. For starting the engine, the generator was used as a starter motor powered by a 60-cell, 236 amp-hr D. P. Kathanode battery. The battery also provided power for lighting and electrical control gear until the engine was started and the auxiliary generator came on line. It was charged by a self-ventilated, 6-pole, 45.9 kW DC English Electric EE909 auxiliary generator that was mounted above the main generator and driven from it. Output of the auxiliary generator was automatically maintained at 135 volts and 340 amps at all engine speeds from 450 to 750 rpm and it was used during normal operation to supply the various auxiliary components described below as well as providing excitation current for the main generator.

From the main generator, current was passed to six axle-hung, 4-pole EE519/1B traction motors, one driving each axle. They were nose-suspended from brackets on the bogie cross-bearers and continuous rating for each motor as installed was 178 hp at 500 amps with a one-hour rating of 200 hp at 575 amps. Although capable of 935 rpm, the motors were governed to 750 rpm, which equated to the locomotive's maximum speed of 93 mph.[23] The motors were arranged in three groups of two. The centre and outer ones of the leading (No. 1 end) bogie were one pair, the inner ones of each bogie the second, and the centre and outer ones of the trailing (No. 2 end) bogie formed the third pair. Within each pair the motors were connected in series, whilst the three pairs were wired in parallel. The armatures ran in roller bearings and drove the axles via single-stage 55:18 spur gears, the ratio being chosen to be close to 3:1 without the same teeth meshing as often as that would have entailed. Cooling of the motors was by forced air ventilation from two English Electric EE905/2E electric centrifugal blowers mounted in the nose compartments of the body, each unit driven from the main generator and cooling the three motors on the adjacent bogie. The air was conducted along flexible ducting to one end of each motor casing and exhausted through mesh covered slots around the casing at the other end.

When track speed reached 32 mph, with the driver's power controller in the next to last of its eight notches, or 42 mph with the controller fully open, field diversion or field weakening of the excitation current to the main generator occurred, which enabled the locomotive to carry on accelerating. Readers who want to know more about this aspect of the traction system will find a simple explanation of it at Appendix C so I won't go any further into it here.

FRAMES

It was decided that the body was going to be a completely separate entity from the frames and would not be used to impart any overall structural strength. This presented the problem of how to make the frames alone sufficiently strong between the bogies to carry the weight of the engine and other equipment whilst allowing the bogies sufficient swing, placing cabs at both ends, and installing a walkway between them. These problems were solved by draughtsmen in the Development Drawing Office run by Eric Langridge, but before starting detailed design work, they had to find out what sort of steel sections could be readily obtained in those austerity days. One of the section's staff was sent to search the stockholdings of steel firms and

The completed frames for 10000 are seen in this photograph taken at Derby Works in 1947. As described in the text, the longitudinal members were made from rolled I-section steel with the centre sections cut and welded. We can tell that the frames are from No. 10000 by the stencilling on the front indicating that they were the first of order 2510. Note the purpose-built frames and brackets on which the locomotives were supported during construction until such time as they were mounted on their bogies.
NATIONAL RAILWAY MUSEUM (DY 35833)

After the frames were completed, they were moved into the diesel erecting shop. The next operation was to fit the main deck plates followed by the 16SVT engine and generator as well as the radiator trunking before commencing installation of the electrical conduits and wiring. This is the stage that had been reached with 10000 when this photograph was taken. On the far side of the main structure was one of the bogies under construction whilst behind it were two of the 'twin motor' 350 hp diesel shunters undergoing repair. In the adjacent bay were several steam locomotives also undergoing repair, including 'Black 5' No. 4843.
NATIONAL RAILWAY MUSEUM (DY 35839)

No. 9 – MAIN LINE DIESEL-ELECTRICS Nos. 10000 and 10001

This photograph was taken from the other end of the locomotive after the boiler, water and fuel tanks, control cubicle, radiators, main fuel tanks and traction motor blowers had been installed. It was first published in a descriptive booklet by English Electric.
ENGLISH ELECTRIC CO., CTY. J. JENNISON

some lengths of deep rolled I-section were discovered.

The side members of the frames were made by cutting and welding these I-sections, the design being such that welds were kept away from the stressed portions. To cater for the inevitable flexing when the frame assembly was loaded, it was made with a camber so that the middle was 3in higher than the ends; when the engine, generators and other equipment was installed it became flat, The structure was completed by cross members onto which the bogies, engine and generator unit, and other equipment were fixed. The attachment plates for the stretchers, etc. had to be machined in order to obtain dimensional accuracy and the only planing machine on which this could be done was in the boiler shop. To get the frames onto the planer, a window had to be removed and the frames moved in and out through the hole and across the bottom yard. While they were in place, a red flag was hung on the projecting end of the frames by day and a red lamp by night, warning people of their presence. Underneath the frames, between the bogies, were the battery boxes. The frame construction was a masterpiece that was due in no small part to the skill and supervision of the welding shop foreman, George Cokayne, and stood throughout the lives of the locomotives as testimony to him and his men.

A main deck plate with drainage gullies ran the full length of the locomotive on top of the frames to prevent fluid leaks or other detritus from above getting onto the traction motors or other equipment below it. It was intended that anything spilled would be collected in the gullies whence it was led into a pipe to a drain cock sited away from the electrics, but this was not entirely successful, as will be described later. Fabricated beams at the ends of the frames carried standard screw-link couplings, vacuum pipes, train-heating pipes, and electrical connections for multiple working. They also mounted Turton & Platt 'No-weld' oval buffers with 16 swg steel tapered fairings outside the casings.

Aluminium floorplates were arranged to provide a continuous walkway from one end of the locomotive to the other, albeit via a somewhat tortuous route. Just so that no one could forget who built No. 10000, its floorplates had the letters 'LMS' repeated thousands of times in the surface rather than being embossed with the more usual diamond pattern.

BOGIES

The bogies were designed by Edward Fox, who had worked in the Carriage & Wagon Drawing Office, and were based on a lightweight welded design he had produced a few years earlier for the Liverpool–Southport electric trains. It so impressed

This view shows 10000 after the Clarkson boiler and associated tanks, control cubicle, radiators, fuel tanks and traction motor blowers had been installed. The No. 1 end blower can be seen at the near corner of the frames with the fuel gauge mountings on the fronts of the main and service tanks and the balance pipe between the two main tanks at the bottom. In the left foreground was a K series 350 hp shunter engine with one of the 'twin motor' shunters at the far side of No. 10000.
NATIONAL RAILWAY MUSEUM (DY 35849)

No. 9 – MAIN LINE DIESEL-ELECTRICS Nos. 10000 and 10001

Ivatt that he tried to have the design patented but, unfortunately for him, drawings had already appeared in the railway press so his attempt failed. As previously mentioned, drawings had almost been completed for two traction motors on each bogie driving the outer axles but frame bogie centre, whilst at the ends of the H arms were raised plates on which the bearing cups for the side bolsters slid. The spherical seatings that engaged in the bearing cups were carried by girder stays fixed between the main locomotive frames. Pairs of double laminated springs transferred weight from the bolsters to a spring plank suspended by swing links from the bogie cross stretchers, from which pairs of coil springs supported equalising beams bearing onto the axleboxes. As with Stanier's side bolster bogies, therefore, no weight was carried by the pivots

This study shows one of the bogies complete with traction motors and wheels having the brake blocks fitted. The sand boxes were built into the corners of the frames but awaited the lids and operating gear. NATIONAL RAILWAY MUSEUM (DY 35851A)

English Electric then decided that they would have to power all the axles. Since the traction motors were standard English Electric items, the cables from them were a standard length to ensure interchangeability. With three motors per bogie, this presented a problem of positioning junction boxes to which the leads could be connected and from which cables ran to the control cabinet. The solution Fox arrived at was to make the bogie wheelbase uneven at 8ft 0in + 7ft 8in and to fit two of the traction motors facing one way and the third in the opposite direction. The inner and middle motors of each bogie were suspended at the outer ends whilst the outer ones were suspended at the inner ends. Centrelines of the motors were offset 2¹⁄₁₆in from that of the bogie frames.

The bogie frames were relatively lightweight structures welded up from ⁷⁄₁₆in thick steel plate and joined by a cross-member of H section in plan that arched over the middle traction motor. In the centre of the crossbar of the H was an oil bath that received the main locomotive

One of the motor bogies, complete and painted aluminium waiting for the installation of traction motors, axles and wheels, is seen in this photograph. In the foreground was the H-plan cross member that arched over the middle traction motor and received the main locomotive frame bogie centre. Two of the raised oval plates on which the bearing cups for the side bolsters slid can be seen at an angle to the ends of the arms of the 'H'. Evident on the bogie are the pairs of double laminated springs that transferred weight from the bolsters to a spring plank and the pairs of coil springs that supported the equalising beams. Next to the bogie was the main structure of No. 10000 with the other bogie beyond it whilst behind was a 'twin motor' 350 hp shunter. NATIONAL RAILWAY MUSEUM (DY 35847)

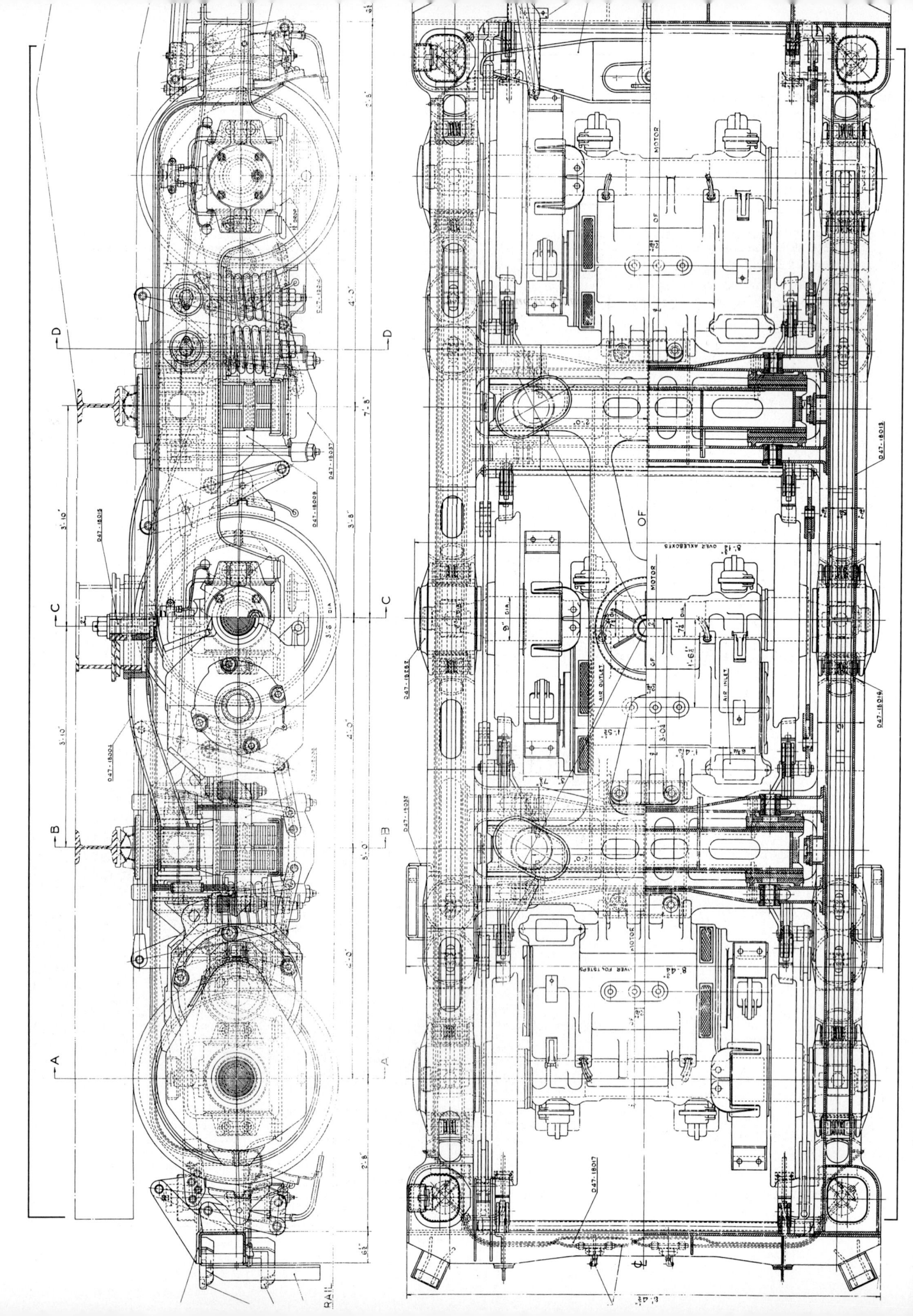

although the tractive effort was transmitted through them. The equalising beams could not be fitted below the axleboxes, as was done with the later steam locomotives, because of limited clearance and they had to be inside the box sections of the side frames.

The Timken roller bearing axleboxes had manganese steel liners in keeping with the latest steam locomotive practice and the 3ft 6in diameter wheels were rolled-steel. Transverse shocks were damped by lugs on the axleboxes that impinged on sprung pads attached to the bogie frames. Short, ladder-style footsteps and supports were attached to the frames below the cab doors and angle-iron lifeguards projected down from the front headstocks. Width over the axleboxes was 8ft 1¾in and over the footsteps was 3in greater. Extreme width over the corners was 8ft 4½in.

Sandboxes were fitted at each corner of the bogies, sanding being effected by electro-pneumatic valves supplied with compressed air by Westinghouse DH25 electric compressors in each adjacent nose compartment. The sand pipes were positioned outside the outer wheels, so sand could be applied to the leading wheels of each bogie in either direction of travel.

No. 10001 was built with four extra stiffening webs fitted vertically to the outsides of the bogie side plates. When 10000 went into Derby Works for repair in July 1948, it too had the extra webs fitted.

BRAKES

The locomotives were vacuum braked, the vacuum being created by two Westinghouse 3V72 vacuum exhausters driven by English Electric EE714/5G motors at the foot of the radiator trunking. When starting a train, both exhausters were used to enable brake release but, once running, one was sufficient to maintain 21in vacuum in the reservoirs and train pipe. Two reservoirs were located side by side between the main-frame longitudinal members above the battery boxes with four 24in diameter brake cylinders — one for each side of each bogie — between the reservoirs and the bogies. All wheels had clasp brakes activated by adjustable linkages to the cylinders. In addition to the vacuum brakes, there was a hand brake wheel in each cab for parking.

D48-18344 — Arrangement of motor bogie

This drawing shows the motor bogies fitted to No. 10000 and even though it has been amended in some respects up to 1957, the extra stiffening webs fitted to the side plates in July 1948 aren't included — these webs were present on 10001's bogies from new. The side elevation on page 22 is split at the centreline: to the right is an external view with some components behind the frames and springs shown chain-dotted; to the left is a section taken inboard of the frame showing the traction motors and details of the suspension. Above the bogie itself is an indication of the girder stays between the locomotive frames together with the spherical bearings and sliding bearings cups of the bolsters as well as the main locomotive frame bogie centre. The plan on page 22 is also split with an external top view above the centreline, some components below the frames being shown chain-dotted. Below the centreline is a section below the top frame plates and through the H-section cross member. The four cross-sections on this page are taken at the places shown on the side elevation. Section A-A is paired with an external end elevation and whilst the wheel, axle, axlebox and frame are sectioned, the traction motor isn't. Section B-B is taken at the centre of one of the bolsters and in addition to the bogie, it shows the locomotive main frame, girder cross stay, bearing and bearing cup. C-C is taken at the middle of the bogie and shows the main locomotive frame bogie centre. Whilst the axle, axlebox and frame are sectioned, the traction motor is merely suggested by a chain-dotted outline. D-D shows sections through one of the coil springs between the spring plank and equalising beams as well as through the traction motor suspension point. External views of the brake, wheel and traction motor are also shown.

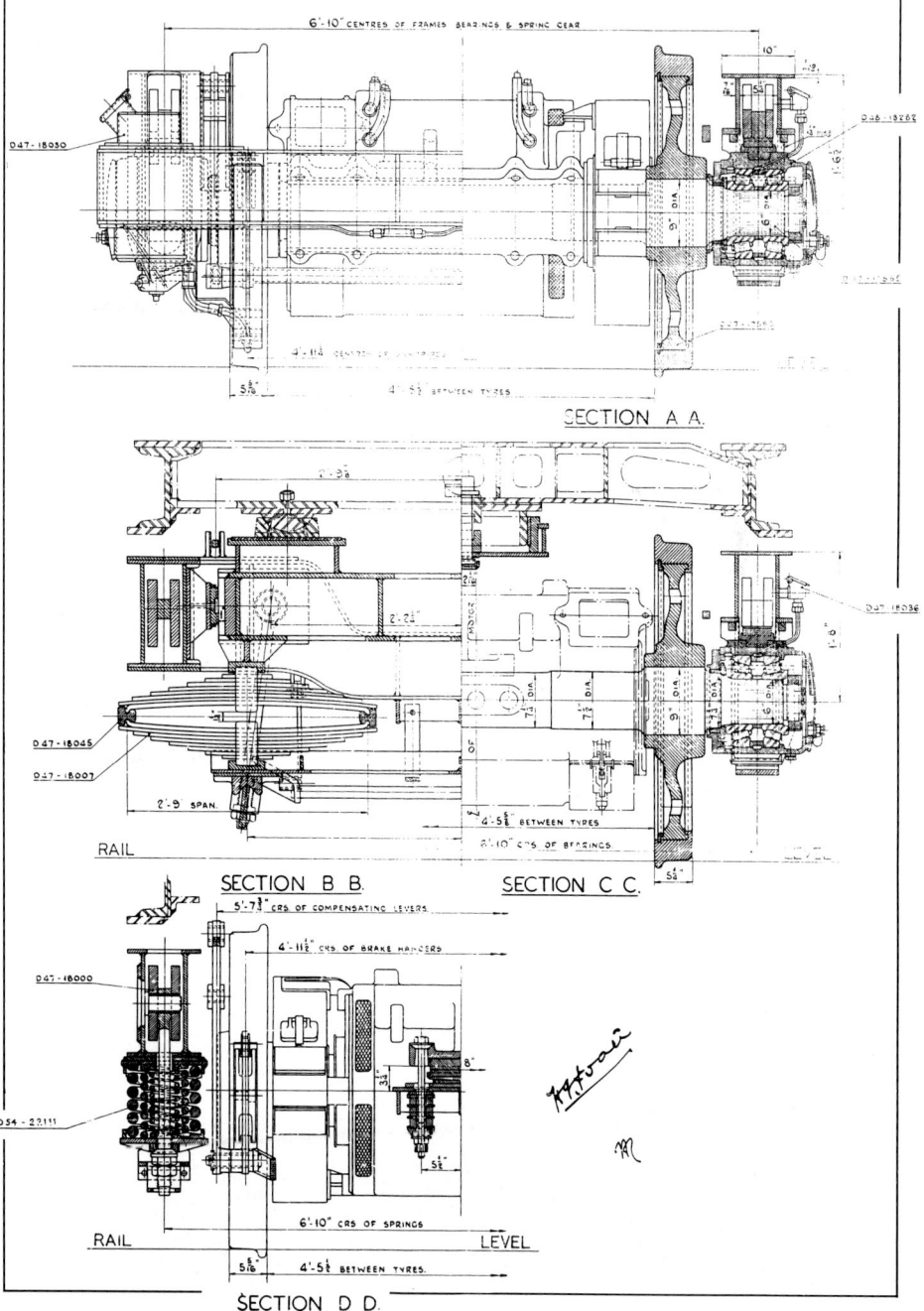

As described in the text, the nose sections were separate structures that were added once the rest of the locomotive was erected and primed. This photograph shows the No. 1 end nose piece ready for fitting to the otherwise complete No. 10000. Note the fuel tank gauges on the front bulkhead and the stencilled 'S' indicating that we are looking at the south end.
NATIONAL RAILWAY MUSEUM (DY 35855)

No. 9 — MAIN LINE DIESEL-ELECTRICS Nos. 10000 and 10001

BODY AND CABS

The main body shell, complete with roof but less cabs and nose sections, was a single structure made up from channel, strip and angle-iron covered with 14 swg steel plates and attached to the frames by two pivots at the bulkheads behind each of the cabs. This arrangement meant that the body took none of the load on the frame and allowed the latter to flex without suffering undue strain. It was built as a separate entity before being split into six sections and fitted to the frames once they were complete with fuel tanks, engine, generators, radiators and trunking, fans, train-heating boiler and tanks, and electrical cupboards and cables all in place. First of all, the end bulkheads were swung into place and fixed to the frames, then the pre-assembled sides were attached to them. Next, the generator flange bulkhead was installed, followed by the roof being fixed to the bulkheads and sides. Not until the entire locomotive was erected and primed were the cab and nose sections fitted. Each of these had a framework of strip, channel and angle-iron, somewhat reminiscent of a rather elaborate greenhouse. They were built at the north end of 10A shop by men from the C&W Works and covered in shaped, 14 swg steel sheets that were panel-beaten on full-width cast-iron forms.

The body sides were detachable to enable sideways removal and re-installation of the engine and generator in the limited headroom of Derby erecting shops after the locomotives were finished. Roof doors were provided so that the exhaust manifold, cylinder heads, pistons, etc. could be examined or removed relatively easily and direct access to the engine compartment was enabled by double doors with recessed handles in the centres of the body sides. Ventilation grilles were provided in the body sides for the radiator, engine, generator, and train-heating compartments. Double windows were set into the side panels above the waist on either side of the engine compartment doors and single ones provided by the generator compartment. Access to the boiler fuel and water tank fillers on 10000 was via oval openings high on the body sides behind the No. 2 cab. There were also two associated recessed hand holds above the waist and two recessed footsteps below the ventilation grilles on each side. The arrangement was then changed so that the tanks could be filled from platform level and 10001 was built without the oval panels, footsteps or hand holds. When 10000 went into Derby Works between 2nd August and 22nd September 1948, it was altered to match 10001 and the oval openings were filled in but the steps and hand holds remained. In later years, the patches over the openings on this locomotive could clearly be seen.

This photograph shows No. 10000 nearing completion with the bogies and the main part of the body in position and the latter primed ready for painting. It was taken from the No. 2 end when the locomotive was awaiting the fitting of its nose sections, driving cabs and engine compartment doors. Note that the body side letters were already in place.
ENGLISH ELECTRIC CO., CTY. J. JENNISON

26   D48-18268 — General arrangement of 1,600 hp diesel-electric locomotive — elevation

Although it has a 1948 prefix, this drawing was dated November 1947 and depicts No. 10000 as built with Clarkson heating boiler, access panels in the body sides for the boiler fuel and water tank fillers, and associated footsteps and hand holds. At this time it was unusual for general arrangement drawings to be produced as they were time-consuming and expensive to prepare, only the best draughtsmen being entrusted with them. Presumably, it was the novelty of main-line diesel traction that prompted this one to be issued. It is an excellent example of the genre, being well detailed but clear and is drawn on similar principles to those used on steam locomotive GAs. The side elevation is as though half the body shell has been removed to reveal the components beneath, which are mainly shown in external rather than sectioned views. Some components, such as the radiators, are shown merely in overall outline without any detail. In general, components behind those nearest to the viewer are shown chain-dotted. The bogies are drawn as though the frames, axleboxes and wheels nearest the viewer have been removed and some components such as the bogie centres are sectioned at their centrelines.

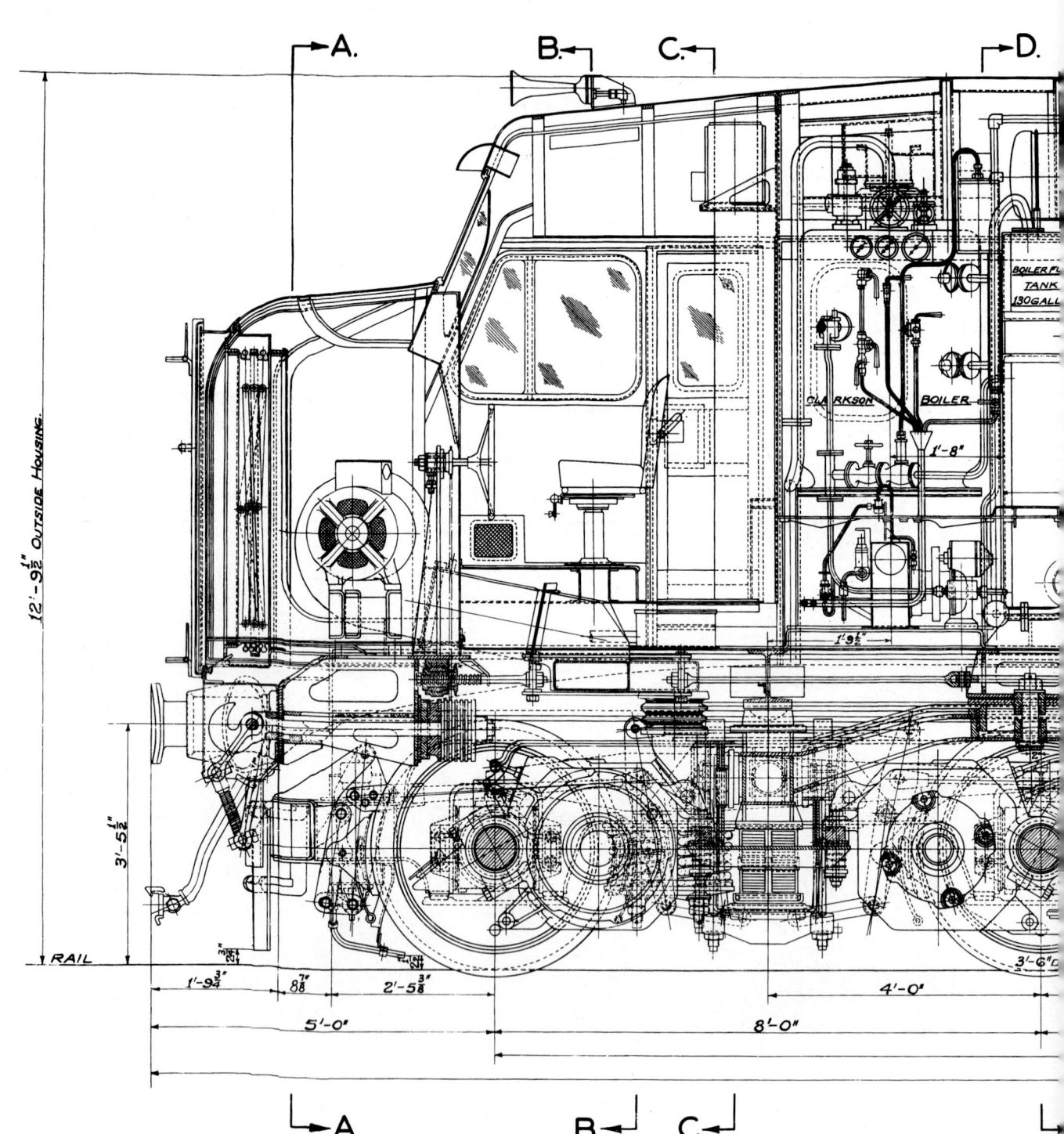

BOGIE CENTRES 35'-6"
TOTAL WHEEL BASE 51'-2"
LENGTH OVER BODY 59'-8"
LENGTH OVER BUFFERS 61'-2"

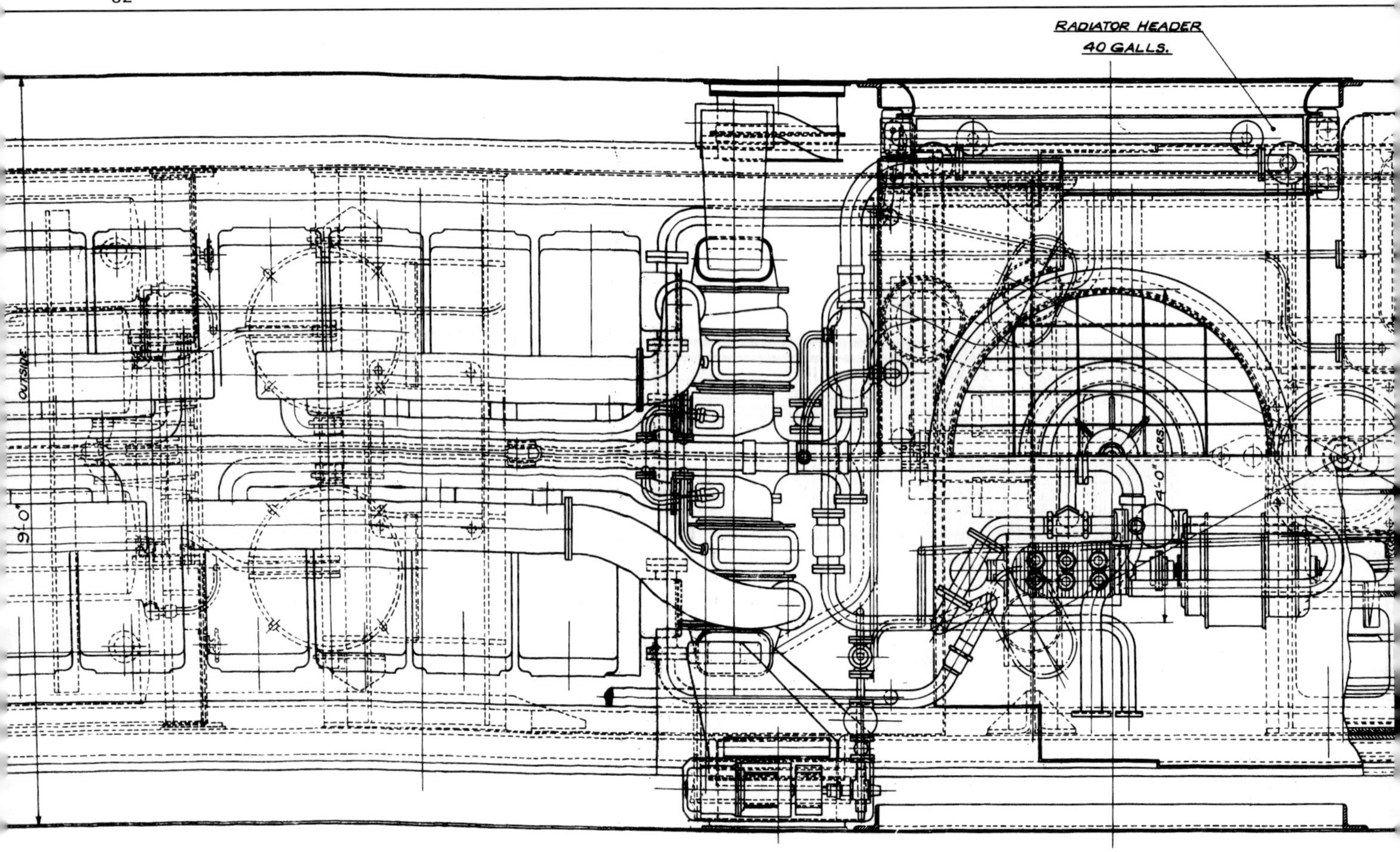

RADIATOR HEADER
40 GALLS.

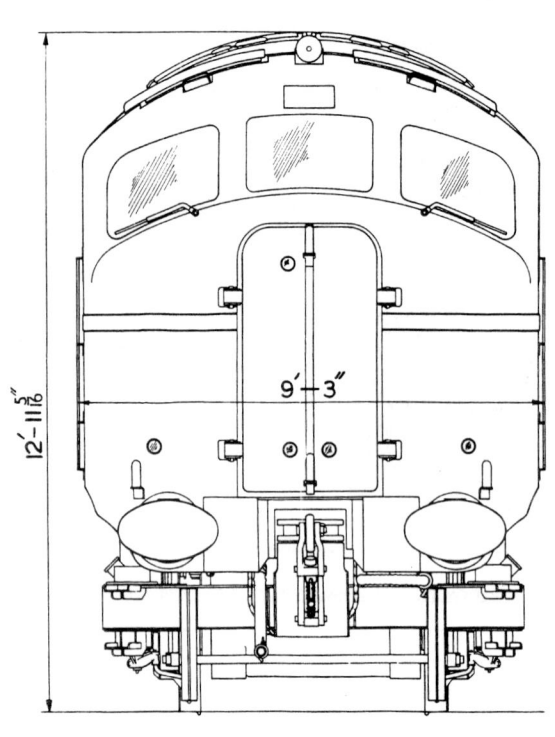

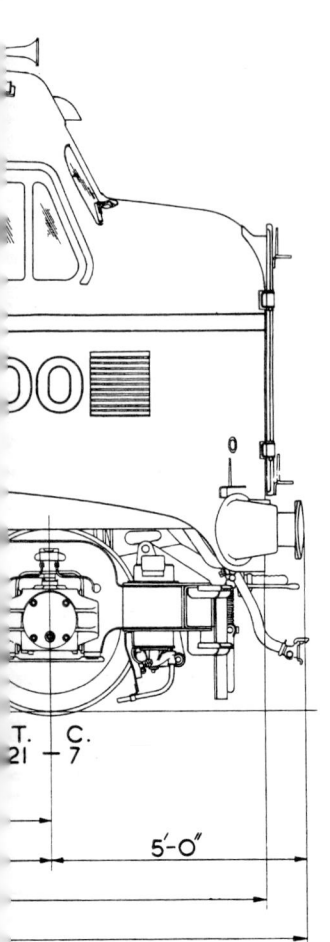

This drawing was prepared ahead of No. 10000's completion as, I believe, part of the LMS publicity drive for its new main-line motive power and should be of particular interest to modellers. The date on the drawing is 9th December 1947 but it must have been altered after that as the bodyside 'LMS' letters with which 10000 was built are not shown whereas BR 'mono-cyling lion' emblems are. The latter, which were not applied to 10000 until March 1951, are shown in the positions that were actually used. Note that the locomotive is shown as built with oval boiler filler access and no bogie stiffening webs.

D47-18222   Main line diesel-electric locomotive

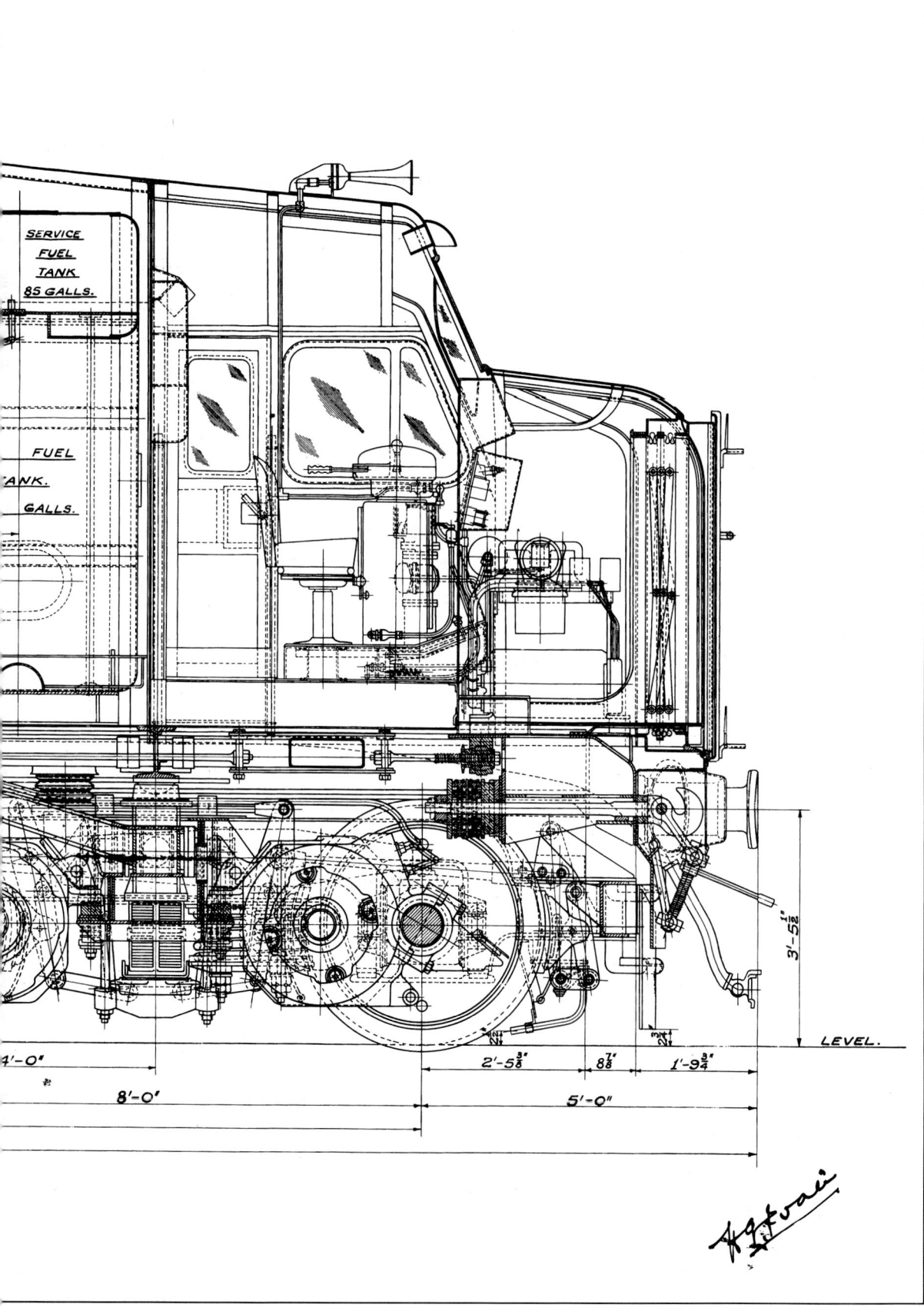

D48-18268 — General arrangement of 1,600 hp diesel-electric locomotive — plan

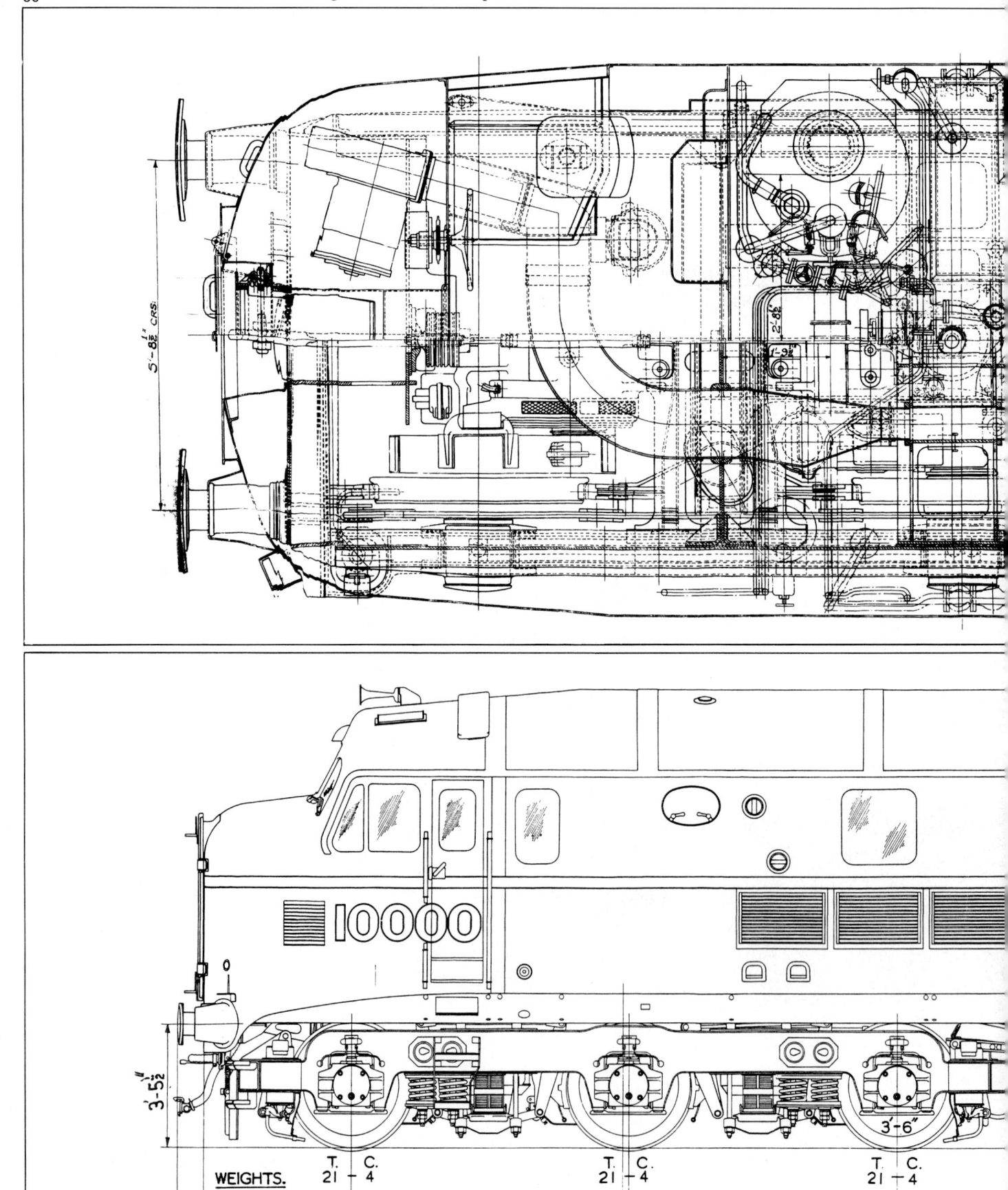

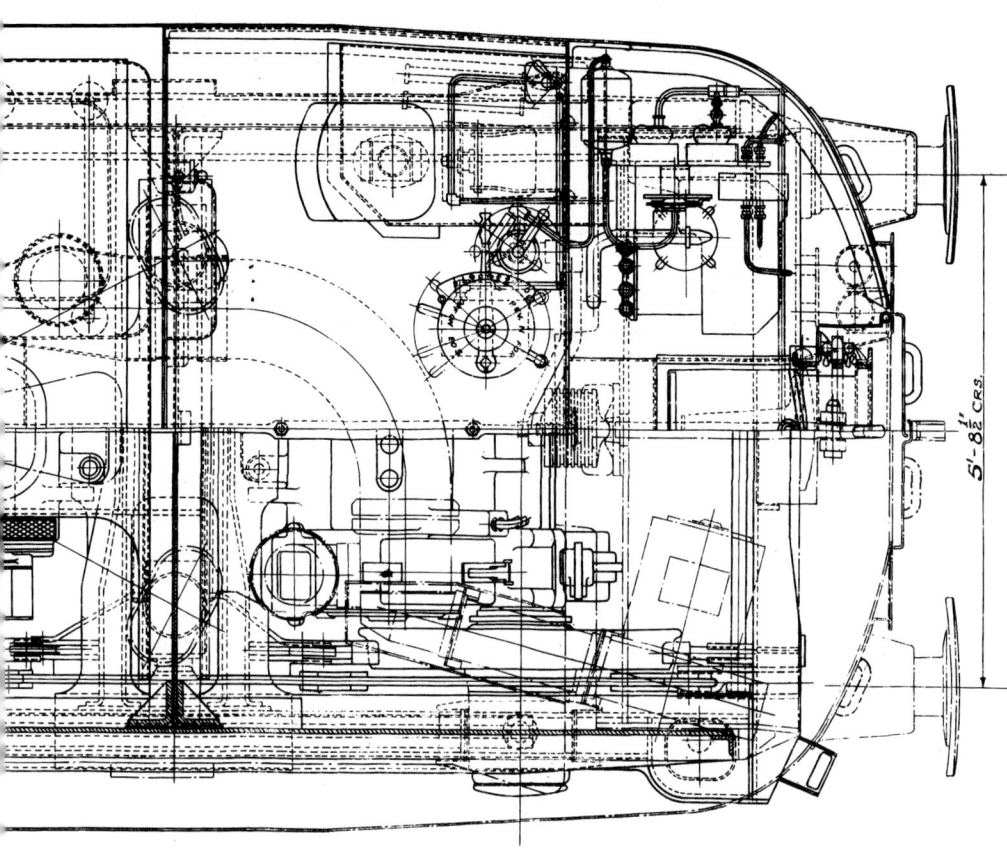

The plan is in several sections. The whole thing is as though the body shell has been sliced off at the waistline and the middle portion shows a simplified top view of the engine and turbochargers. Either side of that it is split above and below the centreline, above being a top view of components mounted on the frames with the main deck plating in place. Below the centreline the deck plating has been removed and we are looking down on components below it. As with the side elevation, some components below those nearest to the viewer are shown chain-dotted.

D48-18345 — General arrangement of 1,600 hp diesel-electric locomotive — end view and section

Drawn at the same time as, and complementing, D48-18268, this drawing shows an external view of one end of the locomotive as well as a section taken just through the nose just behind the gangway connection, i.e. section A-A on the side elevation of D48-18268. The unit on the left of the gangway is one of the traction motor ventilation blowers whilst to the right is one of the Westinghouse electric air compressors. The two trapezoidal shapes above the blower and compressor are the enginemen's instrument panels. The locomotive is drawn with fairings inboard of the buffers over the multiple-unit connectors, which only 10000 had and which were removed in May 1949. Interestingly, it is also shown with grab handles on the waist strip either side of the nose doors and on the doors themselves; these were never present on 10000 and were only fitted to 10001 in 1961. This would suggest that both locomotives were originally intended to have them — why it took fourteen years to get round to fitting them I don't know.

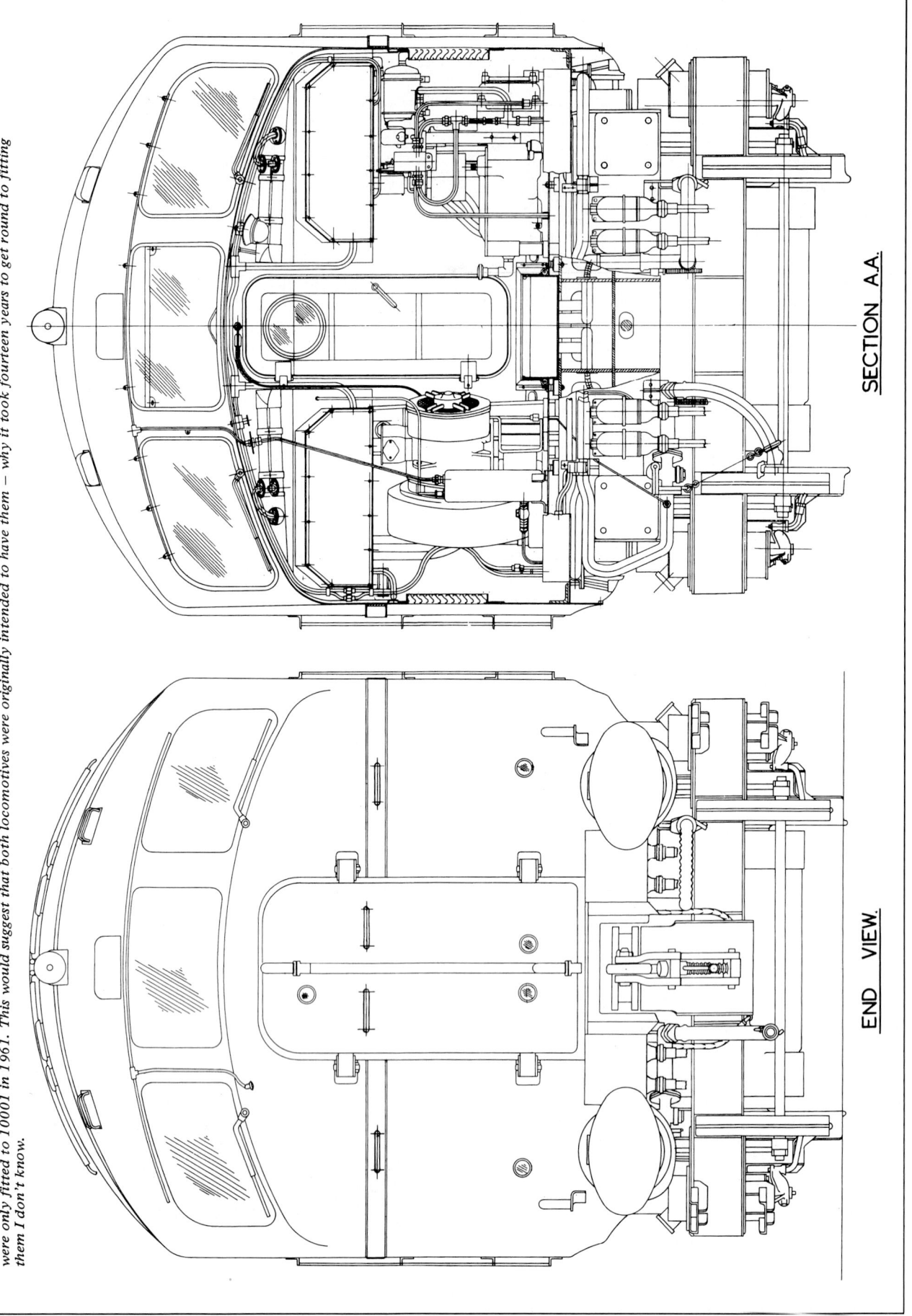

Parts of D48-18346 and 18347 – General arrangement of 1,600 hp diesel-electric locomotive – sections

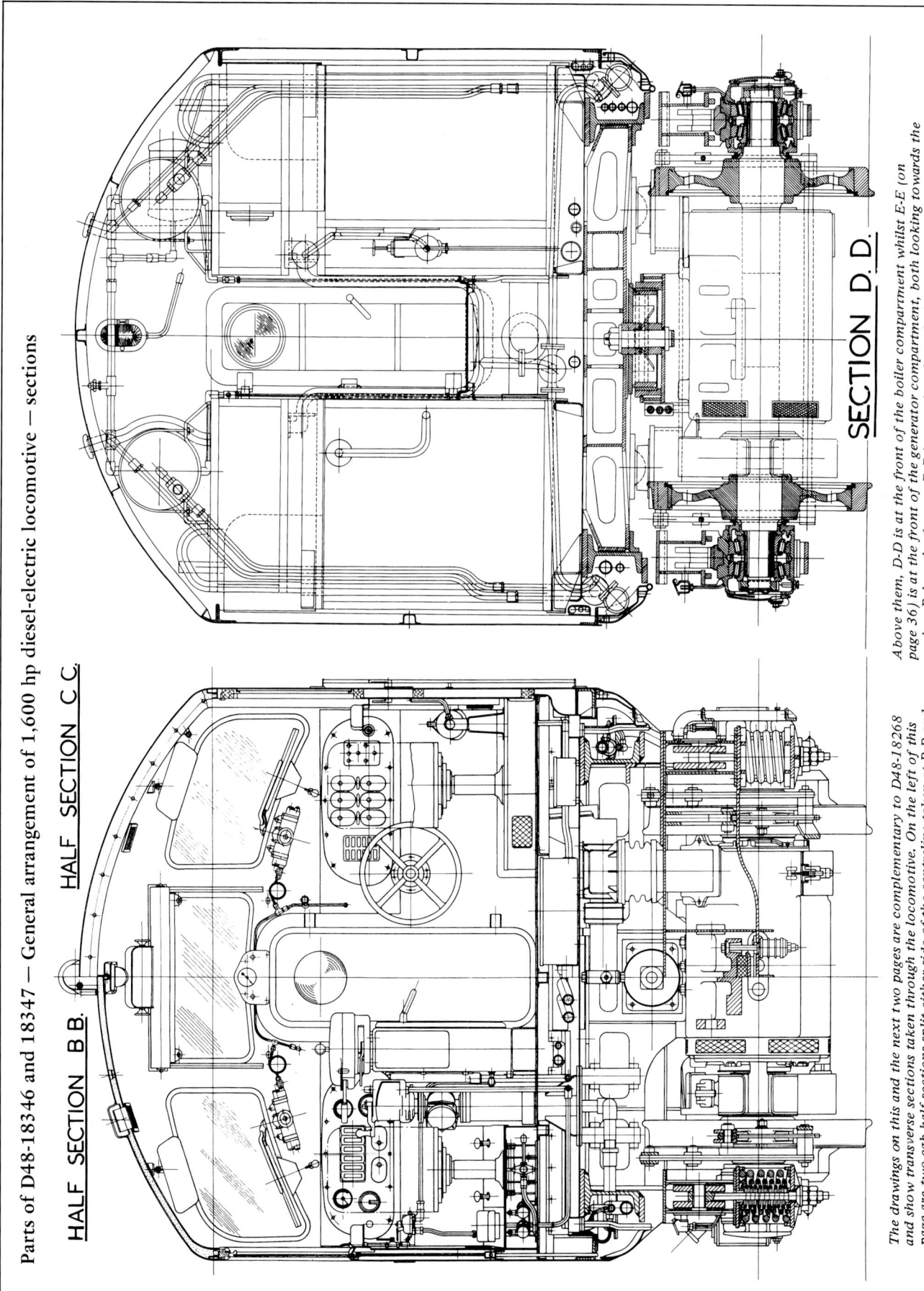

HALF SECTION B.B.

HALF SECTION C.C.

SECTION D.D.

The drawings on this and the next two pages are complementary to D48-18268 and show transverse sections taken through the locomotive. On the left of this page are two cab half-sections split either side of the centreline taken at B-B and C-C respectively on the side elevation of D48-18268 that are actually on slightly different planes above and below the level of the frames. On the right of this page and the left of page 36 are sections that relate to D-D and E-E on D48-18268 and are again on different planes above and below the frames.

Above them, D-D is at the front of the boiler compartment whilst E-E (on page 36) is at the front of the generator compartment, both looking towards the engine. Below the frames, D-D is a section through the centre axle of the No. 2 end bogie, showing the shape of the cast-steel wheels and the arrangement of the Timken roller bearing axleboxes. E-E below the decking is taken between the arms of the transverse H frame and the inner wheels. Both lower sections show simplified external views of the traction motors.

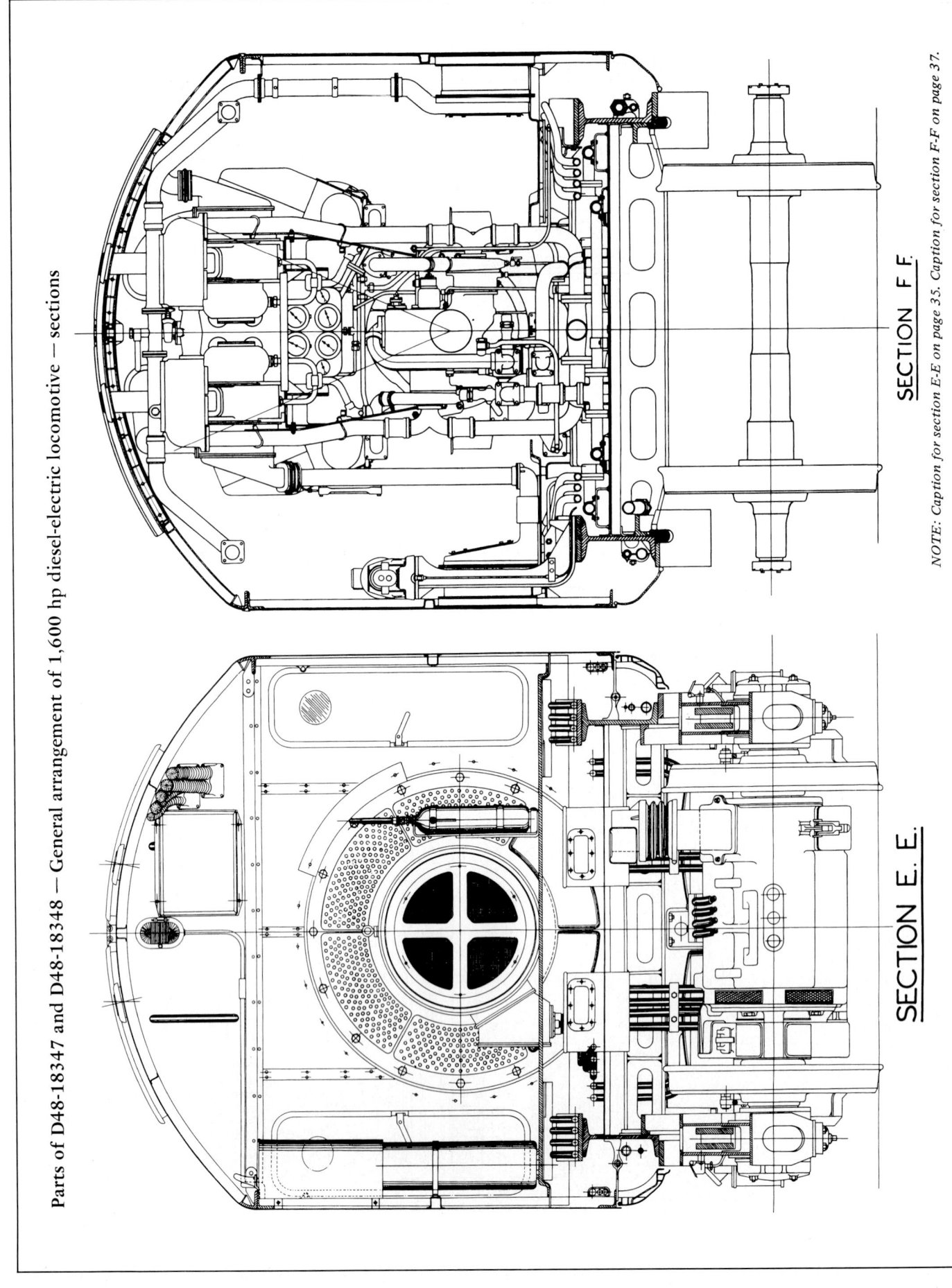

Parts of D48-18347 and D48-18348 — General arrangement of 1,600 hp diesel-electric locomotive — sections

SECTION E.E.

SECTION F.F.

NOTE: Caption for section E-E on page 35. Caption for section F-F on page 37.

Parts of D48-18346 and D48-18348 — General arrangement of 1,600 hp diesel-electric locomotive — sections

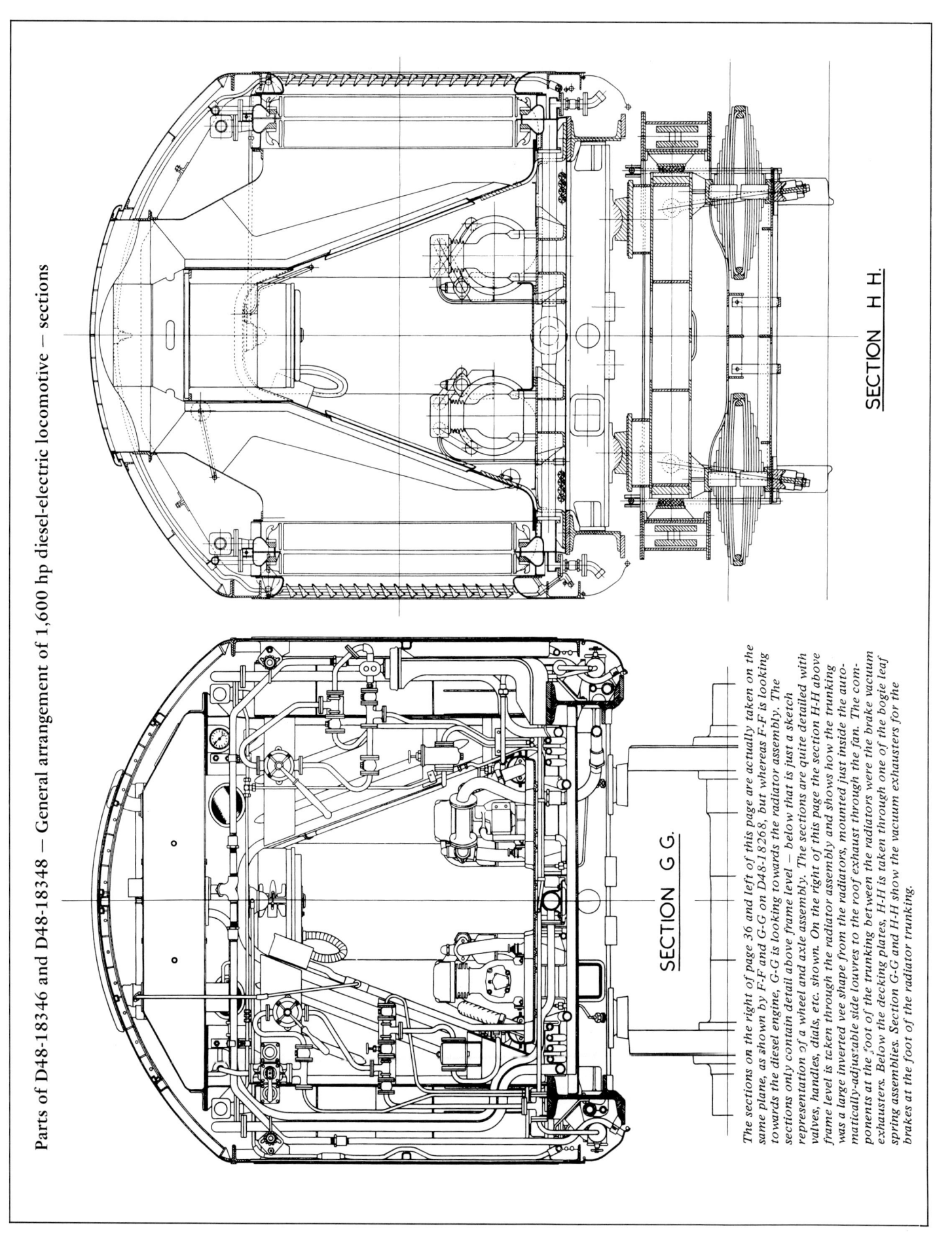

SECTION G.G.

SECTION H.H.

The sections on the right of page 36 and left of this page are actually taken on the same plane, as shown by F-F and G-G on D48-18268, but whereas F-F is looking towards the diesel engine, G-G is looking towards the radiator assembly. The sections only contain detail above frame level — below that is just a sketch representation of a wheel and axle assembly. The sections are quite detailed with valves, handles, dials, etc. shown. On the right of this page the section H-H above frame level is taken through the radiator assembly and shows how the trunking was a large inverted vee shape from the radiators, mounted just inside the automatically-adjustable side louvres to the roof exhaust through the fan. The components at the foot of the trunking between the radiators were the brake vacuum exhausters. Below the decking plates, H-H is taken through one of the bogie leaf spring assemblies. Section G-G and H-H show the vacuum exhausters for the brakes at the foot of the radiator trunking.

D47-17778 – Nosepiece

This drawing shows the structure of the nose pieces that were added to the locomotives once the rest was assembled and primed. The drawing is fairly self-explanatory. Note that the valance sections and buffer fairings were part of the nose assemblies.

Drawing continued on page 40.

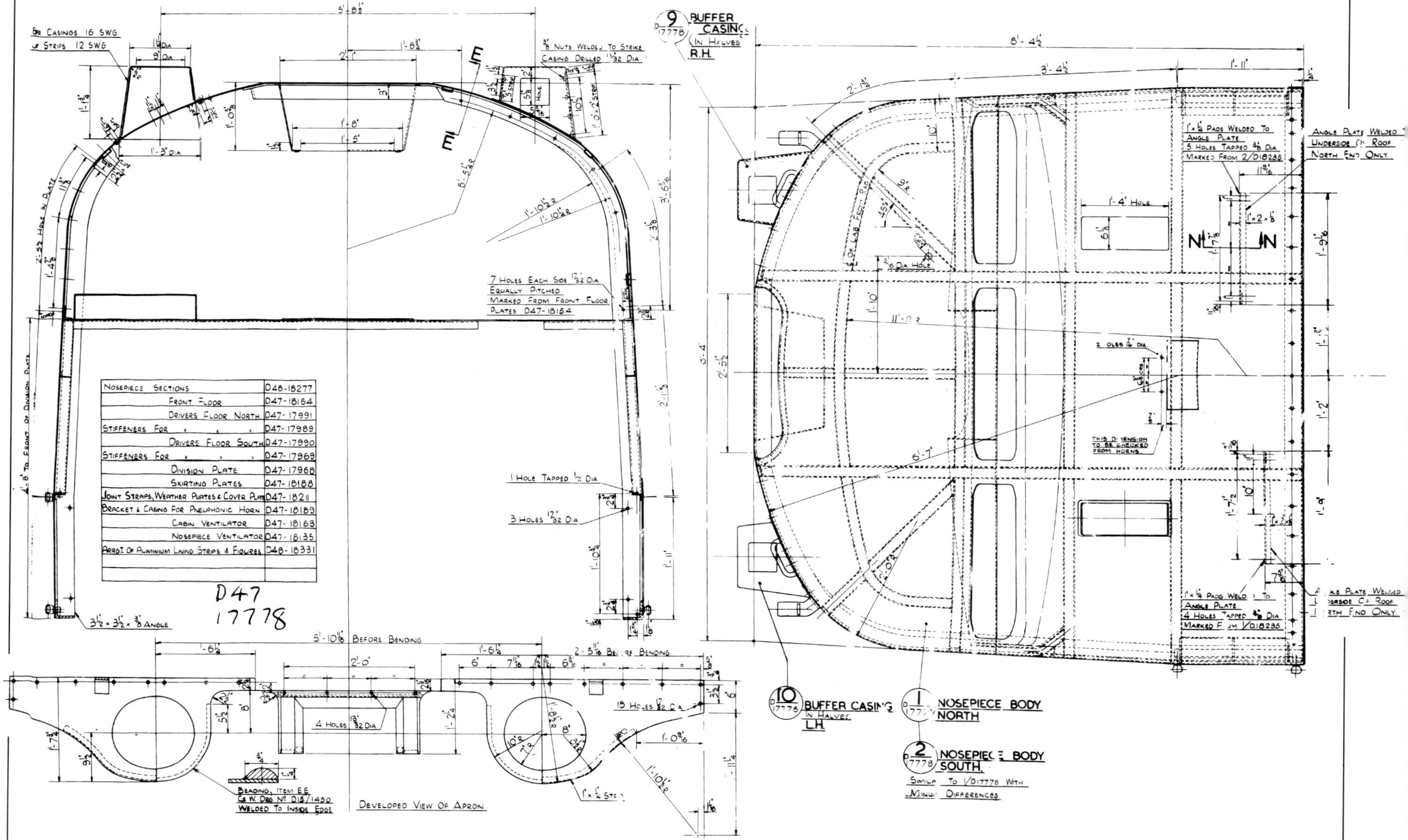

Nosepiece Sections	D48-18277
Front Floor	D47-18154
Drivers Floor North	D47-17991
Stiffeners For " " "	D47-17989
Drivers Floor South	D47-17990
Stiffeners For " " "	D47-17969
Division Plate	D47-17968
Skirting Plates	D47-18188
Joint Straps, Weather Plates & Cover Plate	D47-18211
Bracket & Casing For Pneuphonic Horn	D47-18189
Cabin Ventilator	D47-18163
Nosepiece Ventilator	D47-18135
Arrgt Of Aluminium Lining Strips & Figures	D48-18331

LMS LOCOMOTIVE PROFILES

About halfway down the sides was a horizontal, raised aluminium alloy strip that was continuous right round the body, including the nose sections, interrupted by the cab handrails, engine compartment door handles, radiator louvres, and nose door hinges. Along the lower side extremities from cab to cab were tumblehome fairings that turned under and were fitted in sections hinged along the lower edge so that they could be lowered for access. They were held closed by twist lock fasteners as used in the aircraft industry. Valances started at the cab doors and wrapped round the bottom edges of the nose sections, curving down to cover the buffer beams with cut-outs around the couplings and vacuum pipes. For sound and vibration damping, the entire inside of the body shell and the bulkheads were sprayed with an asbestos compound that would probably give a present-day health and safety inspector a fit. The space in between the double skin of the bulkheads was filled with the same material.

Layout inside the body shell was as follows. Starting at the No. 1 end, the nose compartment contained an air compressor and traction motor blower, air from the blower being fed along trunking to a point above the adjacent bogie and then by flexible pipes to the motors. Immediately behind this was the cab, followed by the fuel tanks, which took up the whole body cross-section except for an access tunnel through the middle. Next came the water radiators and oil coolers on either side followed by the engine. Further along towards the No. 2 end, roughly where the radiators were at the No. 1 end, was a clean-air compartment containing the generators and electrical control gear. Dirt and contaminants from the engine compartment were kept out by sealing off the whole body cross-section at the main generator flange with a bulkhead containing an airtight door. Cooling air for the generators was drawn in through louvres in the body sides via Vokes filters then discharged into the engine room, whence it escaped to atmosphere via roof and side mounted louvres. Another bulkhead with airtight door sealed the clean-air compartment from the train-heating compartment. From the generator and control compartment, the main power cables ran inside 2½ in diameter conduits along the frames to junction boxes above the bogies. The train-heating boiler and its associated oil and water tanks were immediately adjacent to the No. 2 cab, fillers being provid-

D47-17778 – Nosepiece
continued from page 39

ed at the tops of the tanks on 10000 but at platform level on 10001 as built and 10000 when altered. The No. 2 nose section contained another traction motor blower and air compressor.

As well as housing the blowers and compressors, the nose sections incorporated gangways and extendable corridor connections so that the crew could pass between locomotives when working in multiple, although getting through them for anyone of large stature wasn't easy. By using an adapter, connection could also be made with a coach.[24] The connectors were enclosed behind draught-proof doors when not in use. On the outside, lamp or disc holders were fixed to the corners of the nose just above and outside the buffers and to the front of the nose doors, with small electric marker lights adjacent to each one. During daytime on the LMS and then LMR, white discs similar to, but smaller than, those on the Southern Railway were used in place of lamps.

The reason for adopting the nose arrangement with bonnets ahead of the cabs was mainly because of concerns that the crew could become mesmerised by sleepers flashing past immediately below the windscreen. The two cabs were identical in layout and were accessed through inward-opening doors at each side. Adjustable, cushioned seats were provided for driver and fireman (single-man operation was a long way in the future and the term secondman hadn't yet been invented) with individual electric heaters alongside each seat. There were adjustable sun blinds, which were standard Austin car items, for each outer windscreen panel and a roller blind above the centre panel. Ventilators were fitted at the front above the centre windscreen panel and in the roof above each seat. The side windows had droplights and one inch angle on the roof above the windows acted as rain gutters to prevent water running into the cab when they were open. The outer windscreen panels were equipped with blown air demisters as well as air-driven wipers and washers. The wipers could also be hand operated. Other cab equipment included Pyrene fire extinguishers, mounted on the bulkheads, and lockers for the enginemen's property as well as spare fuses, lamps, detonators, etc. Outside were commode-style handrails on either side of the door openings, the ones nearest the nose sections being split above and below the numbers, and what were described as 'pneuphonic' air horns, powered by the same compressor that supplied the sanding gear, were mounted on the roof. The horns produced a single, deep note somewhat reminiscent of the Caledonian and Stanier 'hooters' that was chosen by a group of senior officers from a selection of horns mounted on the roof of the electrical/copper shop — shades of Horwich in the early days of the Grouping!

TRAIN HEATING
The original scheme for train heating was somehow to heat water and make steam by utilising hot exhaust gases from the turbochargers and a considerable amount of time and effort was expended in conjunction with Clarksons, the boiler manufacturers, to this end. Although sufficient heat would have been available when the engine was running at high power, at idle it would not have been possible to keep the heating system operating and so the idea was eventually abandoned.

Instead, the space immediately behind the No. 2 cab housed a Clarkson thimble-tube boiler with its own fuel and water supply that could produce steam at the rate of 1,000 lb per hour at 50 psi. Tank capacities were 130 gallons of fuel oil and 600 gallons of water. The boiler had a Laidlaw-Drew burner with automatic adjustment but basic operation was manual and involved a complicated procedure that had to be followed for lighting it or shutting it down. Actual ignition was simply by applying a hand-held taper to the burner, which was one thing when the locomotive was standing still but another matter when it was travelling at high speed.

All in all, the heating system was the weakest feature of the design. Steam production of a single Clarkson boiler was barely adequate for heating an ordinary passenger train and when the locomotives were working in multiple the two boilers couldn't be used together as the trailing one kept blowing out. Thus, the twins simply couldn't heat the Anglo-Scottish expresses during the winter. Even operating singly, the boilers were dreadfully unreliable and on one occasion No. 10000's fireman had to relight the burner no less than sixteen times in a single trip. This all led to some operating problems as we shall see later. Consideration was given in 1950 to the fitting of Smith-Stone boilers from America but Government restrictions on dollar exchange precluded it. A scheme was then proposed for the elimination of the No. 2 cabs with much larger boilers being fitted in their place but this also came to nothing. Eventually, Job No. 5673 was issued on 1st October 1952 to the financial authority of WO/E2342 for replacement of the Clarkson boilers by Spanner 'Swirlyflow' boilers with a capacity of 2,000 lb per hour. These boilers took their fuel supply from the main fuel tanks and the separate tanks were removed, the space being used to increase water tank capacity to 850 gallons. The alterations increased overall weight by just over three tons. No. 10000 was altered in February 1953 and 10001 modified two months later. In April 1955, No. 10000's new boiler failed and was replaced by another of the same type. Although performance of the Spanner boilers was much better than that of the Clarksons, they were still not completely satisfactory and train heating continued to be something of a problem.

It was also found that the water tank capacity, even after it had been increased, was too small for the Spanner boiler when operating over a long distance so during an intermediate repair ending on 13th October 1955, No. 10000 was fitted with a pneumatically-operated water scoop. It was arranged to pick up from troughs in either direction by actually having two scoops facing opposite ways and connected to a common trunking. At the junction was a loose flap that would be deflected by incoming water and so close off the other scoop, which arrangement was similar to that used on tank engines. Water was conveyed from the scoop assembly to the boiler tanks via rectangular cross-section trunking that could be seen emerging from between the bogie and battery box towards the No. 2 end and entering the lower body sides. At the same time, extra vents were provided in the roof over the boiler compartment, covered by panels that in plan view were truncated triangles and which were raised from the roof at their inner ends.

Rather than being operable from the cab, the scoop had to be worked from the boiler compartment. The fireman would leave the cab when approaching a trough and, when the driver wanted the scoop lowering, he would operate a switch that illuminated an indicator. When the light went out, it indicated that the scoop should be raised. Instructions were issued that care had to be taken not to pick up too much water in case it flooded the boiler, engine and generator compartments with potentially detrimental effects.

No. 10001 was not fitted with a scoop until some time later and I think that it was

DD3930 — Cab controls layout sketch

This Derby Development Section sketch was prepared in 1947 and incorporated in an introductory leaflet issued by the English Electric Company. It shows the cab layout with the driver's position and main control desk on the left-hand side. Comparison with the general arrangement drawings will show the actual positions in the locomotive of most components.

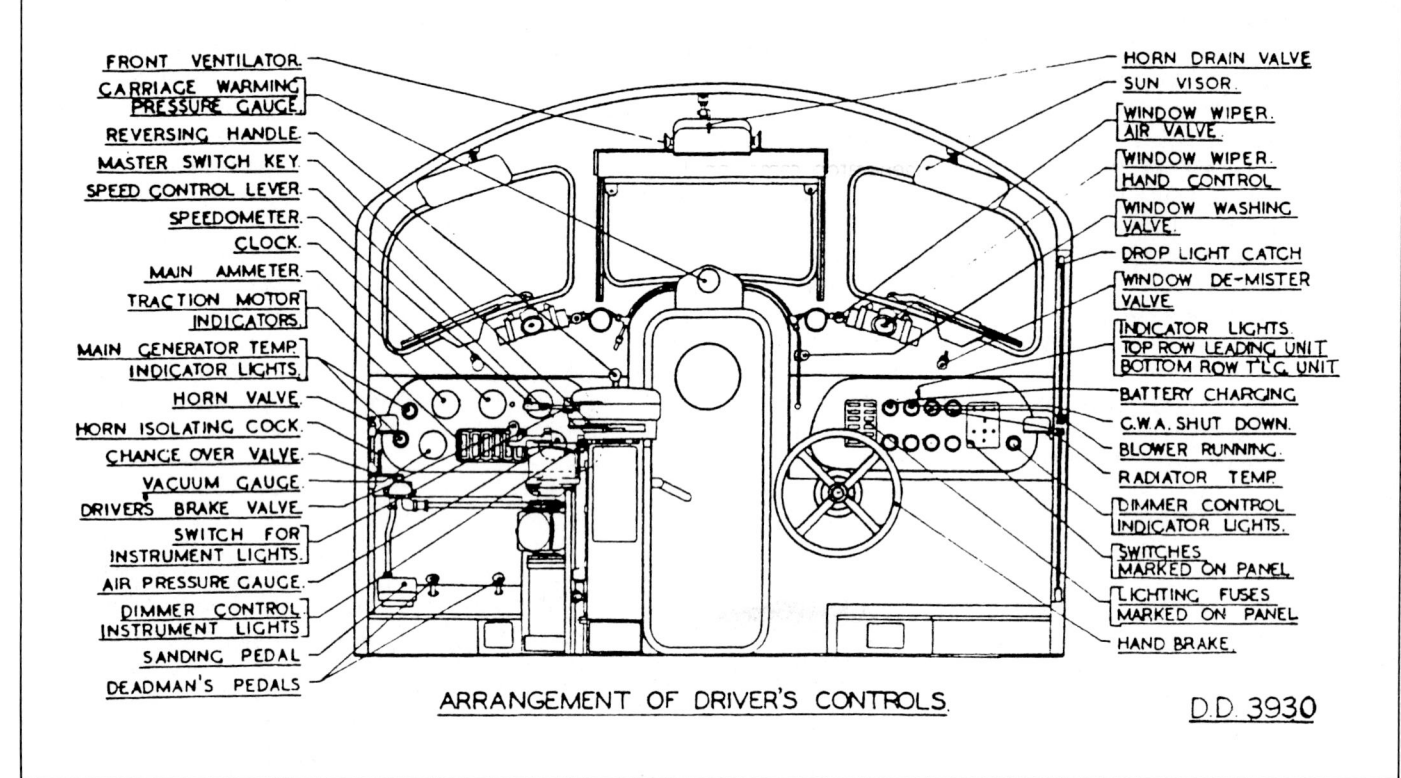

ARRANGEMENT OF DRIVER'S CONTROLS.

D.D. 3930

4th October 1957 before it too was able to pick up water on the move. The trunking was slightly different both in cross-section and curvature from that fitted to 10000 but the locomotive had the same vents and raised roof panels.

CONTROLS AND OPERATION

On the left-hand side of each cab was a control desk with a unit called the master controller, which mounted a master switch for starting and stopping the engine as well as bringing the main generator on line. It also had the main control handle, reverser, and brake handle. The main control handle was flat against the desk and operated around a quadrant with eight notches. There was also a 'dead man's' foot pedal that had to be depressed in order to move the locomotive and kept down at all times when in motion. Should it be released, a relay would close and, after four seconds when working a passenger train or eight seconds with a goods train, would admit air to the train pipe via a restrictor, so applying the brakes steadily. The delay was selectable by a 'Goods/Pass' switch. If the vacuum fell below 9 in Hg, an electro-pneumatic switch in the control cabinet would cut the current to the traction motors.

There were two instrument panels, the driver's one being equipped with a speedometer, duplex vacuum gauge, air pressure gauge, traction motor ammeter, clock, and warning lights for engine, generator and traction motor malfunctions. No. 10001 was fitted when new with a mileometer, one of which was also fitted to 10000 in December 1948. Sanding was operated by a pedal to the left of the dead-man's treadle and switches were provided for the air horn, water scoop, windscreen wipers and windscreen washers.

The fireman's panel on the right-hand side of the cab carried warning lights for battery charging, carriage-warming shut-down, traction motor blowers and radiator temperature, with repeater lights from the slave unit when working in multiple. It also carried switches and dimmer controls for the instrument lights and internal lights in the cab as well as the lighting fuses. Internal lights in all compartments, as well as the external marker lights adjacent to the lamp or disc holders, were powered by a 135 volt circuit from the auxiliary generator and batteries.

Also on the right-hand side of the cab, just to the right of the gangway and below the fireman's panel, was a large handwheel for applying the parking brake on the adjacent bogie. The wheel was connected to the braking system by a chain to allow for bogie movement and when the locomotive was parked, both hand brakes had to be applied. A main fuel tank contents gauge was mounted on the No. 1 cab bulkhead, to the right of the door when facing towards the engine, with another on the front of the service tank above the door.

For obvious reasons, only one control desk at a time could be powered to drive the locomotive. This was achieved by having a master key that could be inserted into a socket at either desk and turned to make that desk live whilst simultaneously locking out the other one. When the locomotives were working in multiple, inserting a key into any of the desks would lock out

No. 9 – MAIN LINE DIESEL-ELECTRICS Nos. 10000 and 10001

all the others. A defective locomotive could be rendered inoperative by operating a cut-off switch in the No. 2 cab. In later years, British Railways introduced a coupling code for diesel locomotives and the LMS twins were identified by red diamonds painted either side of the nose doors just above the valances. When running in multiple, repeater lights, already mentioned, would warn of some failures in the other locomotive. Apart from them, there was a general warning indicator on the operative control desk that remained lit unless a fault developed in the other locomotive (or the bulb failed – making the system fail-safe). If the light went out, the crew had to make their way into the cab of the other locomotive to assess the fault.

To start the engine, the master switch was put to the 'start' position and, when the engine fired, it would be moved to 'engine only'. At that stage there was no excitation of the main generator, which could not be brought on line until a pressure switch in the lubrication circuit was made. Before moving off, the brakes had to be applied, then 21in of vacuum and between 80 and 95 psi air pressure had to be obtained in order to close safety contacts and make the main controller live. Direction of movement was then selected with the reversing handle, the master switch placed in the 'on' position, thus providing excitation current to the main generator, and the locomotive driven using the main control and the brake handle.

Movement of the control handle not only altered the current supply to the traction motors, but also directed the hydraulic engine governor to deliver fuel to the injection pumps at one of three rates and hence rpm. Notches 1 and 2 equated to 425 rpm, notches 3 to 7 gave 600 rpm, and notch 8 resulted in 750 rpm.

The oil supply to the governor came from the engine lubrication circuit, so a drop in pressure greater than a predetermined amount would shut off the fuel supply and stop the engine to avoid damage. Further engine protection was provided by switches in the turbochargers that would shut off fuel if maximum rpm was exceeded or reduce the amount delivered if the boost pressure fell, which would normally indicate failure of one of the turbochargers. The latter situation would also result in an electro-pneumatic switch closing and inserting a limiting resistance in the generator field circuit to reduce the generator output.

The clean-air compartment at No. 2 end contained a control cabinet, in which were the electrical switchgear, electro-magnetic relays and contactors, and electro-pneumatic contactors and switches to transmit the necessary signals to and from the controller, reverser, engine, generator, traction motors and other systems. Instruments in this compartment and the engine compartment monitored the health of engine and electrical gear. Until the main generator came on line, power to the control circuitry was provided by the battery.

The engine and generator compartments were fitted with an electrically-operated fire detection and fixed carbon dioxide extinguishing system. A fire in either compartment would activate heat detectors and cause an alarm bell to ring in the cab, whereupon the driver or fireman could operate the extinguishers.

MODIFICATIONS

Considering that they were experimental machines, 10000 and 10001 seem to have undergone relatively few modifications during their lives. Apart from the change to 10000's train-heating system tank fillers and blanking of the associated access panels as well as replacement of the boilers and provision of water pick-up apparatus on both locomotives described earlier, the only modifications of which I am aware were as follows:

- After initial trials, 10000 reportedly had its fuel tanks strengthened and was fitted with extra inspection covers. I have no other details of these modifications except that 10001 had them incorporated when it was built. No. 10000 was fitted with a mileometer in December 1948 and between February and May 1949, chain drives

This shows the front of the main control frame that was contained within the control cabinet. It was built long before the days of miniaturised electronics. At the top are voltmeters and ammeters for the main and auxiliary generators together with warning lights indicating excessive readings.
ENGLISH ELECTRIC CO., CTY. J. JENNISON

were substituted for the speedometer cable drives on both locomotives. A split bicycle-type chain wheel was clamped to one of the axles and drove a chain to the speedometer generator. The arrangement was not very satisfactory as the chains kept coming off – understandable really at 90 mph.

- As built, 10000 didn't have the jumper connectors for multiple working permanently attached to the front and rear. Instead, the connectors were carried in the cab and plugged in to receptacles at the ends of the locomotive as and when required. Before they could be plugged in, however, portions of the body fairing inboard of the buffers had to be removed. When 10001 was built, the inner portions of the fairings were omitted and the connectors permanently attached to the ends of the locomotive. At the beginning of May 1949, No. 10000 was altered to match.

- When the locomotives were transferred to the Southern Region, some alterations were necessary. Because of the more restrictive loading gauge, overall width was reduced 3in by trimming the cab handrails and grille panels. Extra lamp or disc holders were fitted to the nose sections above the buffers and just below the waist strip with electric marker lights installed next to them. The modifications were carried out at Derby Works to Job No. 5675 with the financial authority of WO/R3402 issued on 26th November 1952. At the same time, copper/lead alloy big end bearings were fitted.

- Some time after November 1953, improvements were made to the fire protection system but I don't have any details.

- During the early part of their stay on the Southern, a further two lamp or disc holders were fitted on either side of the nose doors just above the waist strip. There were, however, no extra marker lights fitted. Although I don't have a specific date for the alteration, I suspect that it took place during heavy general repairs ending in February 1954 for 10001 and May 1954 for 10000. During the locomotives' long spells in Derby Works after returning to LMR metals, these holders were removed by simply cutting them from the small triangular base plates, which were left in place. The other two additional lamp or disc holders and their associated marker lights, however, remained on the locomotives until withdrawal.

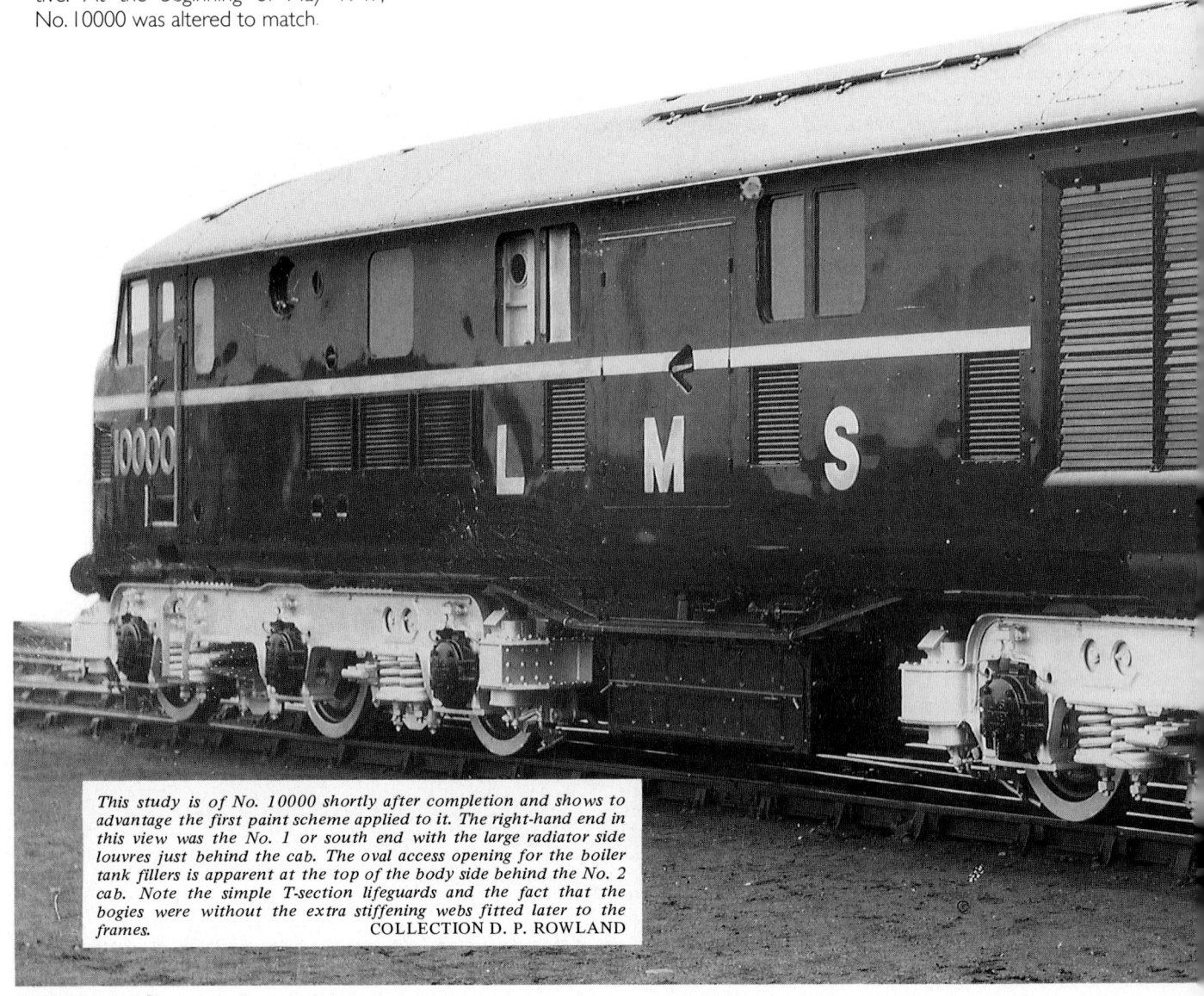

This study is of No. 10000 shortly after completion and shows to advantage the first paint scheme applied to it. The right-hand end in this view was the No. 1 or south end with the large radiator side louvres just behind the cab. The oval access opening for the boiler tank fillers is apparent at the top of the body side behind the No. 2 cab. Note the simple T-section lifeguards and the fact that the bogies were without the extra stiffening webs fitted later to the frames.
COLLECTION D. P. ROWLAND

No. 9 – MAIN LINE DIESEL-ELECTRICS Nos. 10000 and 10001

- Although the main deck plates had gullies to collect spilled diesel oil and prevent it from leaking onto the traction motors and electrical equipment, the arrangement did not provide complete protection and some oil did get through onto the bogies. It then mixed with dirt to form an inflammable goo that from time to time was set on fire by sparks from the brakes. To cure the problem, a fairly major modification was undertaken whereby sealing plates were installed during the locomotives' extended visits to Derby Works in 1956.
- Problems were experienced with internal scaling of the train-heating boiler after the modification described earlier. To counter this, Job No. 5826 was issued on 8th February 1960 with financial authority to WO/R9831 to fit TIA water treatment equipment. No. 10001 was fitted when it was in Derby Works between February and July that year with 10000 following between August and November.
- Job 5830 was issued on 9th May 1960 for the fitting of new speedometers with financial authority under WO/D2550. At the beginning of 1963, however, it was noted as being 'in abeyance' and I doubt whether either locomotive was ever altered.
- In about 1961, No. 10001 had extra grab handles fitted to the corners of the nose sections on the waist strips and to the nose doors just above the strips.

The first time No. 10000 appeared at St. Pancras was with an eleven-coach train plus dynamometer car on 14th January 1948. It was photographed preparing to leave the next day with the same train to Manchester Central before returning to Derby. The Horwich dynamometer car was the first vehicle behind the locomotive. The headcode was an LMS one indicating that the train was operating over the Midland Division with a locomotive on test and the discs showed that it was an express passenger working. Driver Burton can be seen looking out of the cab door and the figure climbing up to join him was George Ivatt. Note the valancing between the coupling and the buffers and the opening at the top of the body side at the far end.

BRITISH RAILWAYS LMR, CTY. D. P. ROWLAND

No. 9 – MAIN LINE DIESEL-ELECTRICS Nos. 10000 and 10001

THE LOCOMOTIVES IN SERVICE

This photograph shows 10000 leaving St. Pancras with its eleven-coach train on 14th January 1948.

BRITISH RAILWAYS LMR, CTY. N. J. WHEAT

Following its emergence from Derby Works, 10000 was subjected to various tests and trials before being sent to Euston on 16th December 1947. It was under the control of driver Burton, who had been given a comprehensive 30 minutes training in the yard before being entrusted with the company's brand new and very expensive machine! At Euston, it was inspected by the Directors before being put on show two days later alongside brand-new Pacific No. 6256 when the latter was named *Sir William A. Stanier FRS*. It then took a five-coach test train to Watford and back before returning to Derby. Although allocated to Camden depot, it was actually being maintained daily at Derby Works and was officially recorded as being on loan there. It undertook a run from Derby to St. Pancras with an eleven-coach train plus dynamometer car – 393 tons in all – on 14th January 1948 with Ivatt in the cab. Ivatt had voiced misgivings about the load but was assured by English Electric representatives that all would be well and so it proved to be. Timings were those applying to a 5XP 'Jubilee' and 10000 maintained time easily, topping Sharnbrook summit at 37 mph and reaching 81 mph between Mill Hill and Hendon. The train left St. Pancras

On 15th January 1948, No. 10000 worked a test train from St. Pancras to Manchester Central and then returned to Derby. This photograph was taken at Millers Dale and shows Driver Burton attending to something on the No. 1 end nose watched by George Ivatt. JOHN DIXON CTY. D. GARNETT

for Manchester Central at 9.00 am the next day with the CMEs of the other BR Regions – Hawksworth, Peppercorn and Bulleid – on board and even though there was no specific attempt made to better the booked times, the locomotive showed some of its promise on sections such as the climb from Millers Dale to Peak Forest when it gained two minutes – an improvement of 20% on schedule. From Manchester, it returned to Derby the same day. Shortly afterwards, English Electric proudly announced that with trains of 400 tons gross, 10000 was capable of over 70 mph on the level, 48 mph on a 1 in 200 gradient and 32 mph on 1 in 100.

The locomotive then went into the Works, where the minor modifications previously described were carried out, and reappeared on 9th February for train heating and braking tests as well as crew training. On 23rd February, it began regular service with the 8.55am up express from Derby to St. Pancras, returning with the 2/15pm down express. Apart from a 40-minute delay because of a fuel blockage on

No. 10000's first day of regular service was 23rd February 1948 when it took the 8.55 a.m. up express from Derby to St. Pancras, returning with the 2/15 p.m. down express. It is seen here approaching Hendon with the eleven-coach up train and it appears that George Ivatt was once again in the cab. Whilst its black paint was still clean and glossy, it can be seen that the silver roof and bogies were beginning to show the effects of being in traffic. Note the boiler tank access in the top of the body side at the far end.
CENTRAL PRESS PHOTOS

No. 10000 was still immaculate in its striking black and silver when photographed at Napsbury on 13th March 1948 with the 7.15 a.m. Manchester–St. Pancras express. Note the oval access for the train-heating boiler behind the leading cab and the valancing panels between buffers and couplings; in September 1948 and May 1949 respectively, these features would disappear. A close examination also reveals that the bogie side frames were without the extra stiffening webs fitted in September 1948. E. D. BRUTON

No. 9 — MAIN LINE DIESEL-ELECTRICS Nos. 10000 and 10001

From 6th April 1948, No. 10000 was diagrammed for two return trips per day between Derby and St. Pancras with express passenger trains. On the 15th of that month it was photographed entering St. Pancras at the head of the 8.55 a.m. from Derby.
D. W. BLACK
CTY. H. J. BLACK

its inaugural run, the locomotive maintained time or bettered it with trains of up to 390 tons and its acceleration was noted as brisk. From 15th March, 10000's diagram was extended to include a return working from Derby to Manchester Central — 7/06pm ex-Derby and leaving Manchester at 12.10am. The following day it failed at Loughborough but was back in service on 19th March.

From 6th April it was rostered to another return Derby – St. Pancras run rather than going to Manchester, departure times being 7/37pm from Derby and 11/50pm from London. Weekly mileage on this diagram was 3,084. Throughout this time, performance was noted as being slightly better than a 5XP in good mechanical condition and the pre-war schedule of 99 minutes from St. Pancras to Leicester was maintained with ease.

When 10001 was nearing completion, 10000 was taken into Derby Works one Sunday so that the two locomotives could be tested for working in multiple. Fred James witnessed the tests in the paint shop and told me how, despite the care that had been taken, it was uncertain whether things would work as advertised. Perhaps the last-minute snag with 10000's wiring the previous December was still fresh in several minds. To cater for the unexpected, the locomotives were positioned about twenty feet apart and connected by extension cables from the jumpers. To

During their early service, the twin diesels were always assured of keen attention when they appeared in public either single or working in multiple. This occasion in June 1948 when No. 10000 was setting back onto the 2.15 p.m. Manchester express at St. Pancras was no exception. Note the front valancing inboard of the buffers and the oval boiler tank access high on the side behind the No. 2 cab.
KEN NUNN COLLECTION (7522)

During its early days, 10000 was frequently seen on the Midland main line between Derby and St. Pancras. This photograph, taken sometime between the locomotive entering service and having its side access to the train-heating boiler blanked off in August 1948, shows it at Luton with an express passenger train.
A. CLARKE

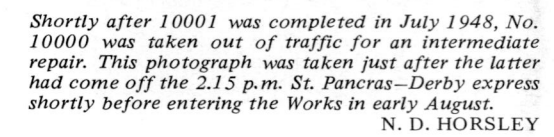

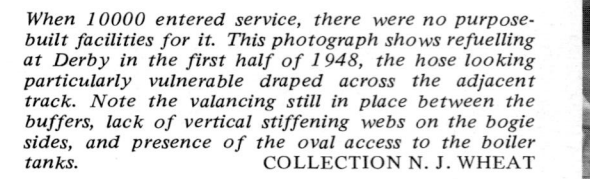

Shortly after 10001 was completed in July 1948, No. 10000 was taken out of traffic for an intermediate repair. This photograph was taken just after the latter had come off the 2.15 p.m. St. Pancras–Derby express shortly before entering the Works in early August.
N. D. HORSLEY

When 10000 entered service, there were no purpose-built facilities for it. This photograph shows refuelling at Derby in the first half of 1948, the hose looking particularly vulnerable draped across the adjacent track. Note the valancing still in place between the buffers, lack of vertical stiffening webs on the bogie sides, and presence of the oval access to the boiler tanks.
COLLECTION N. J. WHEAT

No. 9 – MAIN LINE DIESEL-ELECTRICS Nos. 10000 and 10001

No. 10001 was photographed shortly after being completed in Derby Works. The main visible differences from 10000 – lack of openings at the tops of the body sides behind the No. 2 cab, valancing inboard of the buffers, and no bodyside lettering – are apparent in this view. The other external difference, which was the extra stiffening webs on the bogie frames, can also just be seen.
COLLECTION REX CONWAY

When 10001 was completed, the twins undertook multiple working trials around Derby, including some runs over the Peak Forest route. This is the only photograph I have seen taken at Millers Dale during those trials and although of somewhat indifferent quality, it shows that 10001 was noticeably cleaner than 10000.
JOHN DIXON, CTY. D. GARNETT

everyone's relief, the pair moved off in the same direction at the same rate. When working in multiple, they were normally coupled with their No.1 ends outward, which was meant to optimise cooling airflow to the radiators.

No. 10001 finally emerged from Derby Works in July 1948 and, after testing, it took part with 10000 in further trials in the Derby area and over the Peak Forest route, working in multiple. In August, it replaced 10000 on the Derby–London trains and the latter went into the Works for an intermediate repair, having run a creditable 51,300 miles. No. 10001 was also allocated to Camden but both locomotives were recorded officially as being on loan to Derby. They were still being maintained on a daily basis at Derby Works during this time, mainly because nowhere else had the capability to carry out anything more than very minor rectification or adjustment on them. Even so, there were no proper refuelling facilities, despite the Chief Operating Manager's recommendation in December 1947 that a special siding with such facilities be established at Euston, and it was fortunate that they didn't need their tanks filling for every trip.

By 1st October both locomotives were available for traffic and they left Derby for Camden, where they were used on the West Coast Main Line for crew training until commencing their first long-distance runs working in multiple from Euston to Carlisle on the 1/00pm Glasgow express of 5th October. The load as far as Crewe was 530 tons gross, then four coaches for Blackpool were detached and the load reduced to 390 tons. Time was not only maintained easily but the schedule was bettered throughout and the two locomotives took their train over Grayrigg at a minimum of 58 mph and then past Scout

1st October 1948 was the first time that both locomotives were available for regular traffic. The first long-distance train that they worked in multiple was the 1.00 p.m. Euston–Glasgow express of 5th October, which the diesels took as far as Carlisle. These pictures show them leaving Euston with the 530-ton train and it can be seen that the nose doors between the locomotives were open with the gangways connected. By this time, No. 10000 had received extra stiffening webs on its bogie frames and the oval openings in its body sides had been filled in, both alterations being visible here.
T. J. EDGINGTON

No. 9 — MAIN LINE DIESEL-ELECTRICS Nos. 10000 and 10001

This photograph shows the twins passing over Bushey troughs with the 1.00 p.m. down Glasgow express on 5th October 1948. As can be seen, they were coupled with their No. 2 ends together, which was the usual way they were paired.
BRITISH RAILWAYS LMR
CTY. D. P. ROWLAND

Green at 49 mph on the 1 in 75 up Shap. A number of delays were encountered as well as there being few places where the train was allowed to exceed 75 mph and if allowance is made for the stops at Rugby and Crewe, the net time from Euston to Carlisle on a non-stop basis was 4 hr 49 min. This was only six minutes longer than the pre-war 'Coronation Scot' schedule with 315 tons gross, fewer permanent way slacks and less speed restriction. Details of the timings on this run were as shown in the table.

Five days later, 10000 failed and was taken to Derby Works, whereupon 10001 returned to the Derby–St. Pancras and Manchester Central workings. In November, both locomotives were allocated to Willesden and returned to West Coast Main Line trains working in multiple. For the next ten months they continued to undertake such duties unless one of them needed attention at Derby, when the other one would transfer to hauling Derby–St. Pancras and Manchester trains whilst waiting for its twin to re-enter traffic.

	Distance (miles)	Schedule (minutes)	Actual running time (minutes)	Net running time (minutes)	Net gain on schedule (minutes)
Euston–Rugby	82.6	93	86.5	80.5	12.5
Rugby–Crewe	75.5	90	90	75	15
Crewe–Carlisle	141	183	160.75	136.5	46.5
	299.1	366	337.75	292	74

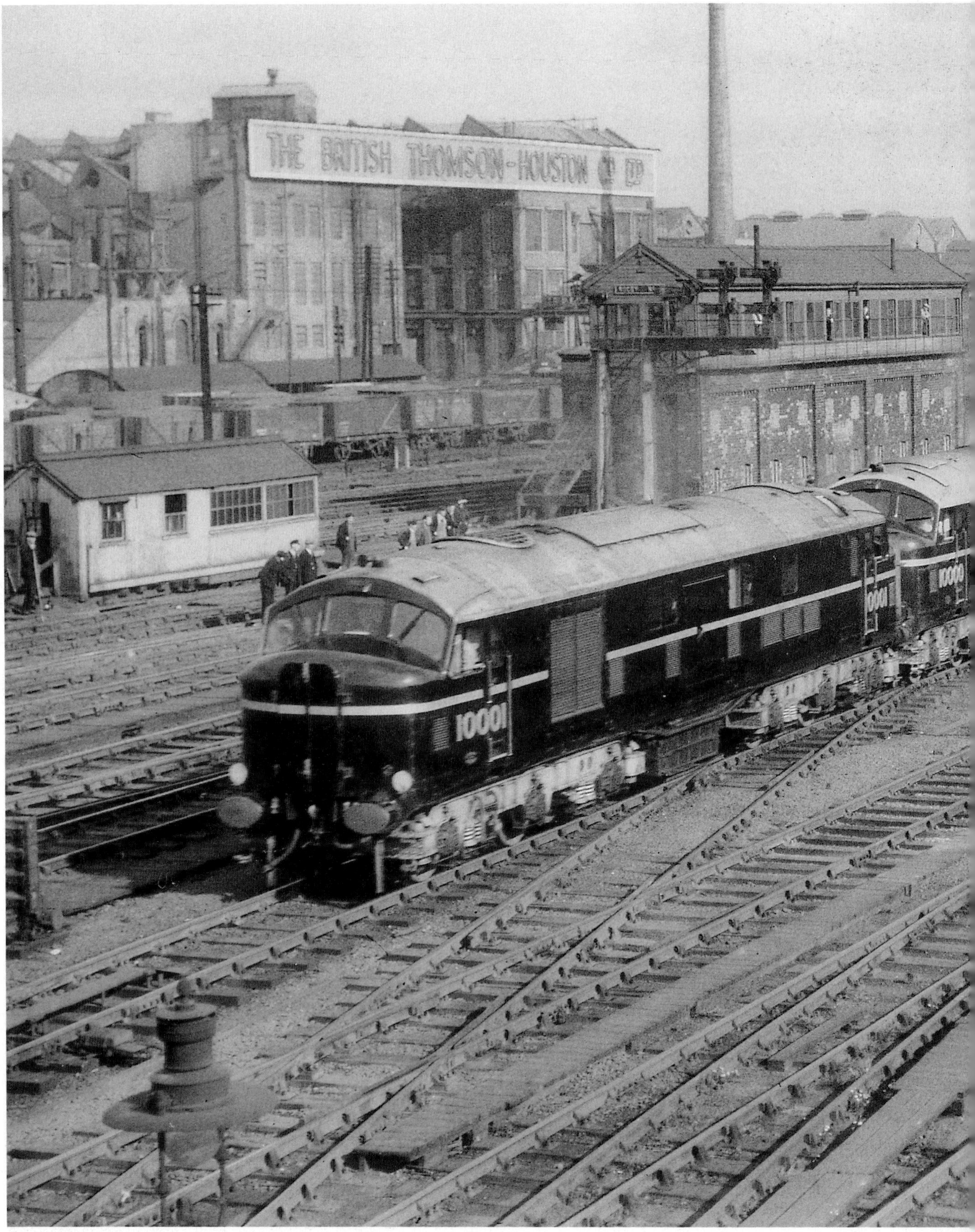
THE BRITISH THOMSON-HOUSTON Co LTD
10001
10000

No. 9 – MAIN LINE DIESEL-ELECTRICS Nos. 10000 and 10001

In October 1948, after No. 10000 had emerged from Derby Works in September with the original access to the boiler fillers blanked off and extra stiffening webs added to the bogie frames, the two diesels began working in multiple on the West Coast Main Line. While 10000 had been in the works, 10001 had been working on London–Derby trains and, as can be seen in this photograph of the locomotives leaving Rugby with a down express, its roof was less clean than 10000's.
COLLECTION R. J. ESSERY

This view shows the diesel twins about to depart from Euston on their first run with the down 'Royal Scot' on 1st June 1949. Not only had the locomotives been specially cleaned for the occasion, but it is apparent that their bogies had been repainted.
COLLECTION J. JENNISON

Following their inaugural 'Royal Scot' run of 1st June 1949, the twin diesels returned to Euston the following day with the 10.00 a.m. up 'Royal Scot'. Prior to departure they were photographed with a crowd of admirers.
R. S. CARPENTER

No. 9 – MAIN LINE DIESEL-ELECTRICS Nos. 10000 and 10001

During this time, the previously described problems with the train-heating boilers were beginning to manifest themselves and didn't bode well for the future in terms of winter passenger train haulage.

On Wednesday 1st June 1949, the twin diesels hauled the 'Royal Scot' non-stop from Euston to Glasgow, omitting the halt at Carlisle Kingmoor usually employed to change footplate crews. The train consisted of no less than sixteen coaches, including a twelve-wheeled dining car, and weighed over 530 tons gross, the extra two coaches over the normal formation being added to accommodate British Railways and English Electric staff as well as press representatives. Two of the notable figures on the train were R. A. Riddles and H. G. Ivatt. With this load, the locomotives managed to crest Shap at 38 mph and Beattock at 36 mph. A special corridor connection adapter was used between the No. 1 end of 10001 and the leading coach so that during the journey, the official guests could be allowed to visit the locomotives. Between Penrith and Carlisle the footplate crew changed over on the run and the train returned to Euston the next day as the 10.00am up 'Royal Scot'.

From then until the middle of September the two diesels continued to work in multiple, at first making the return trip from Euston to Carlisle each day but later operating out of Glasgow with the up 'Royal Scot' and returning with the 545 ton, 9/05pm down sleeping car express. Both runs were non-stop, totalling over 800 miles, and it was the first time that locomotives could be diagrammed to take a return working between London and Glasgow in a day. Daily mileage was approaching that of the NYC Harmon–Chicago workings referred to earlier and

The first time the 'Royal Scot' was diesel hauled was on 1st June 1949 when 10000 and 10001 took the down train from Euston to Glasgow. The following day the engines returned with the 10.00 a.m. up 'Royal Scot' and were photographed passing Wembley. At this stage they did not carry the 'Royal Scot' headboard. COLLECTION K. NUNN

In the summer of 1949, the two diesel-electrics were photographed at Grayrigg with the up 'Royal Scot' before the well-known straight train headboard was introduced. The locomotives were still quite clean, if a little dusty, and the coaching stock was carmine and cream.
P. RANSOME-WALLIS/NATIONAL RAILWAY MUSEUM

During the winter of 1949/50 the main-line diesels were employed on freight trains, firstly to test them on such duties and secondly because the poor train-heating system made them unsuitable for working passenger trains in cold weather. A typical working was the 2.55 p.m. Camden–Crewe fitted freight of over 500 tons seen in this photograph about to leave behind 10000 in January 1950. The disc headcode indicates an express freight train partly fitted with the automatic brake operative on not less than one-third of the vehicles. The lamp above the left-hand buffer was not part of the headcode. Note the third nought split in half by the cab door and the makers' plate below the numbers. Several contemporary observers have commented on the fact that the diesels were allowed to get quite dirty while employed on freight turns and this picture seems to confirm it. The blanking plate fitted over the body side opening by the boiler tanks can be seen.

BRITISH RAILWAYS LMR, CTY. D. P. ROWLAND

No. 9 – MAIN LINE DIESEL-ELECTRICS Nos. 10000 and 10001

the locomotives' ability to carry out such work seemed to bode well for the high mileage that diesel-electrics would have to run in order to justify their first cost.

For the following nine months the locomotives worked separately. At first, they remained on passenger duties such as Euston–Blackpool expresses of 460 tons gross, which was no mean feat for a 5P, as well as venturing north of the border as far as Aberdeen. As winter set in, however, they were removed to freight duties both for trial purposes and because of the earlier troubles experienced with the train-heating system. A typical working was the 2/55pm Camden–Crewe fitted freight with about 520 tons gross and a booked average speed of 45 mph over 156 miles. Given the rolling resistance of the stock used, this was a creditable performance. The return working was normally a Crewe–Willesden freight and while the schedule was easier, the load frequently exceeded 600 tons and occasionally approached 800 tons with a maximum booked speed of 53 mph. On one occasion when normal freight working was disrupted by fog, 10000 took a 60-wagon coal train of 1,100 tons gross from Rugby to Willesden running at unfitted speeds. Despite the traction motor gearing being optimised for fast running, the locomotive managed the train without problem and

A month after the previous photograph No. 10000 was again in charge of the 2.55 p.m. ex-Camden. This view shows it passing Bushey troughs north-bound wearing the same headcode and with its roof looking decidedly grubby.
BRITISH RAILWAYS LMR

The twins were quite at home working semi-fitted freights, or 'Maltese' as they were known to railwaymen because of the Maltese Cross symbol that denoted them in the working timetable. In this photograph, No. 10000 is seen in charge of a Crewe–Brent 'Maltese' in April 1950 near Watford.
KEN NUNN COLLECTION (7865)

Between May and September 1950, the twins worked the up 'Royal Scot' and down sleeper between Glasgow and London. They are seen here passing Tring with the former in July of that year with 10001 leading, which seems to have been the more usual configuration at the time, and mounting the attractive, straight 'Royal Scot' headboard. By this time, both locomotives were beginning to look a little careworn and the previously bright silver and black livery was in need of refurbishment, which happened when they went for heavy general repairs the following November.

BRITISH RAILWAYS LMR, CTY. R. J. ESSERY

No. 9 – MAIN LINE DIESEL-ELECTRICS Nos. 10000 and 10001

The first time 10000 and 10001 worked the 'Royal Scot' was 1st June 1949 and apart from their time on the Southern region, they continued to do so from time to time into the late 1950s. This photograph shows them at Beattock with the up 'Royal Scot' in August 1950, still wearing their original black and silver livery and, although it is difficult to see, 10000 still had its 'LMS' letters on the body sides. Note the absence of valancing inboard of the buffers – a feature of 10001 as built and 10000 after May 1949 – and the indicator discs worn instead of lamps to indicate the train description, in this case express passenger. No. 10001 was still in as-built condition whereas the oval openings in 10000's body sides had been filled in, extra stiffening webs had been added to its bogie frames, and the centre valancing had been removed inboard of its buffers.
AUTHOR'S COLLECTION

sustained speed up the 1 in 330 at Tring cutting was 25 mph.

During the following summer and winter, 10000 and 10001 repeated the same cycle as before, i.e., multiple working between Glasgow and Euston, usually with the up 'Royal Scot' and down sleeper, from May 1950 and then fitted freights and other goods duties from September because of their train-heating problems. Recorded mileage for 1950 was 99,366 for No. 10000 and 97,474 for 10001, of which some 69,000 had been accumulated in just four months from May to August with the Scottish expresses averaging 472 tons tare. Not bad, I feel, for a couple of experimental machines that didn't have the benefit of a properly set-up spares and maintenance organisation. At this stage, fuel consumption since the locomotives entered service equated to 1.2 miles per gallon; whilst working in multiple with 500 tons tare, it was about 1.43 miles per gallon for each locomotive and whilst operating singly with 400 tons tare between Euston and Blackpool, it was about 0.9 miles per gallon.

On 28th November that year, both locomotives entered Derby Works for their first heavy general repairs, 10000 emerging on 9th March 1951 and 10001

No. 10001 is seen here emerging from the tunnel at Elstree with an express passenger train in the autumn of 1950. A short while later, in November that year, it went into Derby Works for its first heavy general repair. As is evident from the photograph, by this time the locomotives had been allowed to get quite dirty and the once striking black and silver livery was distinctly shabby.
COLLECTION N. E. STEAD

on 10th April. The time taken to carry out heavy general repairs was extremely lengthy compared with that for the average steam locomotive but that was really unavoidable. Whereas the progressive repair system meant that steam engine components, including major ones such as boilers and possibly even frames, were exchanged for refurbished items rather than waiting for the originals to be repaired, this simply wasn't possible with the main line diesels.[25] Being the only ones of their kind, without a comprehensive spares backup and depending on rectification by English Electric staff of the engine and electrical gear, it is understandable that repair times were greatly extended.

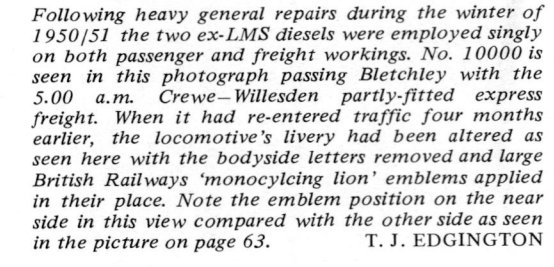

Following heavy general repairs during the winter of 1950/51 the two ex-LMS diesels were employed singly on both passenger and freight workings. No. 10000 is seen in this photograph passing Bletchley with the 5.00 a.m. Crewe–Willesden partly-fitted express freight. When it had re-entered traffic four months earlier, the locomotive's livery had been altered as seen here with the bodyside letters removed and large British Railways 'monocylcing lion' emblems applied in their place. Note the emblem position on the near side in this view compared with the other side as seen in the picture on page 63. T. J. EDGINGTON

On Saturday 30th June 1951, No. 10001 was in charge of the 5.05 p.m. Euston–Blackpool express stopping at Wigan North Western. This picture shows the locomotive with its crew and a group of admirers during that stop. From left to right, the three foreground figures were fireman Norman, driver Frank Brooker and a young man called Norman Harvey.
R. F. ROBERTS

No. 9 — MAIN LINE DIESEL-ELECTRICS Nos. 10000 and 10001

In 1951 the locomotives were used pretty much as before, although they were to be seen on freight as well as passenger workings in the summer. Because they had been in the Works for over two and three months respectively at the start of the year, mileage was down at 87,251 for 10000 and 77,008 for 10001. Single locomotive workings included Euston–Crewe, Euston–Liverpool and Euston–Blackpool trains, often loaded to over 450 tons and involving daily mileage of 700 plus. For a few days in June, 10001 was rostered singly to London–Glasgow trains, loading to nearly 500 tons.

The diesel twins had a less happy year in 1952 and their reliability was quite poor. The trial period on the London, Midland Region had finished and it is possible that they were getting less favourable attention than before in what was a relatively hostile environment at steam sheds. Whatever the reasons, availability suffered and although 10001 managed a semi-respectable 70,732 miles, 10000 only achieved 46,240.

Early in 1953, it was decided to concentrate all the BR experimental diesels on the Southern Region. As well as 10000 and 10001, this included the LMS-inspired 10800 plus the Southern Region's 10201 and 10202 as well as 10203 when the latter entered service. After undergoing the previously described alterations, 10000 arrived at its new home depot of Nine Elms on 2nd March 1953 and 10001 joined it seven weeks later. At first they were used on a variety of duties but from the middle of May the most common were Waterloo–Exeter, Waterloo–Weymouth and Waterloo–Bournemouth returns with express passenger trains. Other workings included Brighton–Tunbridge Wells passenger trains when running in after repair, Waterloo–Salisbury and Exeter–

Judging by the headcode and vehicles behind it, No. 10001 was heading an express freight train, pipe-fitted throughout, with the automatic brake operative on not less than half the vehicles when it was photographed at Tring cutting in May 1952.   C. R. L. COLES

Despite their poor record while on the Southern Region, the twins were sometimes used on the prestigious trains. In this photograph, 10000 is seen passing Esher with the 12.30 p.m. down 'Bournemouth Belle' from Waterloo on 9th August 1953. At this time, the extra disc holders above the waist strip had yet to be fitted and there was no indication of power classification.
R. F. ROBERTS

No. 10000 is seen in this photograph about to leave Bournemouth with a Pullman train, its status indicated by the Southern headcode using one of the extra lamp or disc holders fitted in 1953. The picture was taken before the locomotive went into Brighton Works for a heavy general repair on 5th October 1953, hence it still had large BR emblems on the sides without any power classification shown and didn't have the extra lamp or disc holders on either side of the nose doors.
COLLECTION D. HILLS

No. 9 – MAIN LINE DIESEL-ELECTRICS Nos. 10000 and 10001

Templecombe passenger turns, and Exeter–London evening milk trains.

Their time on the Southern Region was not a happy one. During 1953 their reliability sank to its nadir, failures were common, and although they worked such prestige trains as the 'Royal Wessex' and the 'Bournemouth Belle' singly, they also spent a lot of time at Stewarts Lane depot or in Brighton and Eastleigh Works. Running during 1953 was officially described as 'poor'. Towards the end of June, 10001 went into Brighton works for another heavy general repair from which it didn't emerge until February 1954. No. 10000 followed it in October 1953 and didn't re-enter traffic until the following May. Even allowing for the delaying factors previously discussed, the time it took to repair the locomotives was excessive and suggests that they spent a lot of it merely waiting for someone to get around to dealing with them. During these repairs, the locomotives were both uprated to a nominal 1,750 hp by adjusting the racks that controlled the injector pump output and thus putting extra fuel into the cylinders.

In April 1954, the 2,000 hp diesel No. 10203 entered service and claimed much of the attention previously given to the LMS twins. By the end of the year they had been taken off the prestige services and were restricted to such workings as Waterloo–Salisbury ordinary passenger trains. Even taking into account the delay in

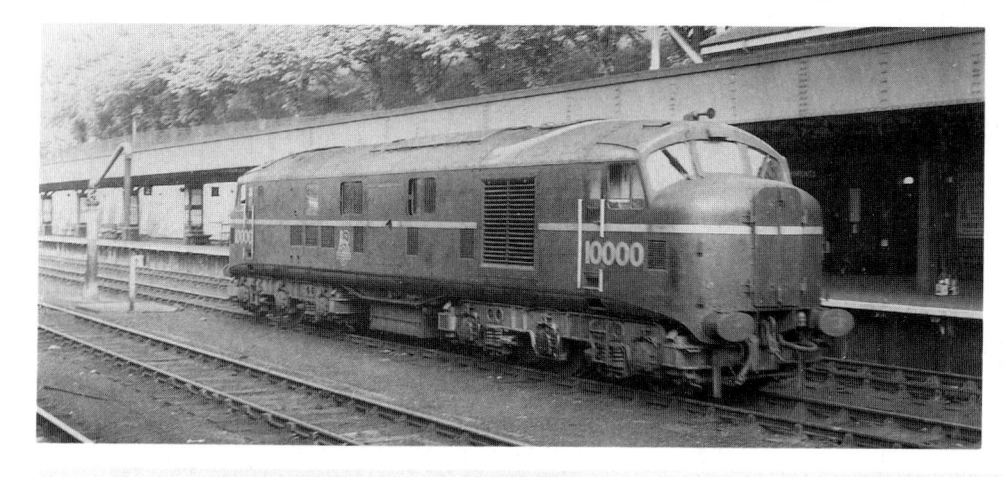

This photograph shows 10000 during its sojourn on the Southern Region before extra disc holders were fitted adjacent to the nose doors, small BR emblems were applied and the power classification was stencilled above the numbers, all of which were probably done in May 1954.
R. H. G. SIMPSON

Extra lamp or disc holders and marker lights were fitted to the nose sections of the locomotives before they were sent to the Southern Region in the Spring of 1953 and a further two added either side of the nose doors in 1954. They are apparent in this photograph of 10000 at Weymouth about to depart with the 5.50 p.m. Waterloo express in June 1954. It can also be discerned that the BR crest on the side was the smaller variety applied in 1954. Less obvious is the fact that the commode handrails either side of the cab doors were modified to protrude less because of the more restricted loading gauge. Note how much bigger were the Southern indicator discs compared with those used on the LMR.
KEN NUNN COLLECTION (8409)

A couple of months after its return from the Southern Region, 10000 was photographed north of Rugby with an express of carmine and cream stock on 6th July 1955. Since being built, extra stiffening webs had been fitted to its bogie side frames and the oval access to the heating boiler on its body sides had been blanked off. The cab handrails and grille panels had been trimmed back to suit the SR loading gauge and extra lamp or disc holders had been fitted to the nose sections above the buffers either side of the waist strip, those below having electric marker lights next to them. Livery was still black and silver but the LMS letters had long gone and the smaller variety of BR emblems were displayed on the engine compartment doors below the waist strip. Power classification 6P 5FA was shown above the numbers in 2in cream Gill Sans transfers. AUTHOR'S COLLECTION

In March 1950, No. 10001 was photographed near Berkhamsted with a Crewe–Willesden hauling what was known to railwaymen as a 'Maltese' – an express freight train in which the continuous brake was fitted to less than one-third of the vehicles but on at least four immediately following the locomotive. The same headlamp code, however, could also indicate a train with the continuous brake fitted to only four vehicles or fewer, the two classifications attracting different bell codes. Three months after this picture was taken, the headlamp codes were revised and that seen here would only refer to the latter category. The locomotive was in 'as built' condition wearing its original livery without any indication of ownership. It had only been back in traffic for a couple of weeks following nearly four months in Derby Works and was notably clean.
E. D. BRUTON

No. 9 – MAIN LINE DIESEL-ELECTRICS Nos. 10000 and 10001

returning the locomotives to traffic from heavy general repair, mileage for 1954 was disappointing at 41,393 for 10000 and 49,391 for 10001.

During the winter of 1954/5, it was decided to transfer all the main-line diesels to the London Midland Region and 10001 was seen back at Camden on 14th March 1955 having come out of a light casual repair at Brighton ten days earlier. It was officially transferred during the week ending 2nd April along with 10000, which emerged from Brighton Works on the first of the month also following a light casual repair. After working Euston–Bletchley locals, the twins and their Southern counterparts were put onto Anglo–Scottish and Manchester turns but availability suffered through maintenance problems as well as a lack of trained crews.

The situation with all the pioneer diesels was far from satisfactory during 1955 but it

On 21st October 1955, No. 10000 was stopped for some defect and entered Derby Works the following day for a non-classified repair to rectify it. The locomotive was still in full 'Southern' condition with no less than seven disc holders at each end and showing 6P 5FA power classification. Light reflections on the side show where the oval access panel to the original boiler tanks had been filled in. The water pick-up trunking fitted during the repair from which the locomotive had emerged a week earlier can be seen entering the lower body side just behind the near bogie, as can the extra vents in the roof above the boiler compartment. The raised panel covering the vents, however, was not in place.
W. POTTER COLLECTION, CTY. KIDDERMINSTER RAILWAY MUSEUM

This photograph shows No. 10001 under repair in Derby Works between June and September 1955 following its return from the Southern Region the previous March. As described in the text, both locomotives spent a lot of time in the Works in 1955 and 1956, as did the ex-Southern Railway diesel-electrics that joined them on the LMR. One of the latter is in the background of the picture and illustrates the size of an English Electric 16SVT engine. The extra lamp or disc holders and marker lights fitted for Southern Region operation can be seen, the right-hand of the two holders adjacent to the nose doors being visible between the hinges. Note the stencilled 6P/5F Southern Region power classification above the number and the makers' plate below it.
COLLECTION D. HILLS

This photograph was taken on 4th March 1956 during 10000's lengthy stay in Derby Works. It shows that although the locomotive had been out of traffic for eight weeks, it had not even been stripped down completely. Its centre roof section had been removed and lifting bars attached to the frames ready for removal of the bogies. At this time, steam locomotives undergoing heavy general repairs only spent an average of 4½ weeks out of traffic but the diesels lacked spares and were therefore incompatible with the progressive repair system.
B. WEBB, CTY. E. M. JOHNSON

No. 9 – MAIN LINE DIESEL-ELECTRICS Nos. 10000 and 10001

The locomotives only ran with yellow roofs and orange and black lining for less than a year. Their appearances with the 'Royal Scot' when thus painted were limited to a few days in November 1956 and during the early summer of 1957. This view shows them in charge of the down 'Royal Scot' near Shap summit sometime between May and July of 1957 when 10000 was fitted with water pick-up apparatus and altered roof profile at the No. 2 end whereas 10001 was unmodified – this was the situation whenever the twins ran in multiple during their 'yellow period'.

COLLECTION R. J. ESSERY

wasn't completely the fault of the locomotives. Lack of proper, clean maintenance facilities needed by diesel-electrics, unfamiliarity at running sheds, and lack of trained personnel all had a detrimental effect and the condition of Nos. 10000 and 10001 gradually deteriorated. By the end of the year, it became obvious that they needed a lot of attention and both went into Derby Works for their third heavy general repairs, 10000 on 7th January 1956 and 10001 a day later. This time their stay at the Works was even longer than before and it wasn't until 24th August that 10001 re-entered traffic, followed on 21st September by 10000.[26] One of the major improvements carried out at this time was to the sealing plates as previously described.

At this time it was decided to de-rate the engines back to 1,600 hp but, when they were tested during adjustment of the injector racks, it was found that not much more than 1,100 hp could be obtained. Investigation revealed that the power reduction was caused by severe pitting of the valves and seats in the fuel pumps. After a complete overhaul of the pumps, the nominal horsepower was set to 1,650. As a result of the inordinate amount of time taken to repair the locomotives, their annual mileage was down to 22,909 and 21,414 respectively.

Dennis Monk relates the story that towards the end of their stay in the Works, the CME, J. F. Harrison, rang Freddie Simpson, who was Works Manager, to ask why the locomotives were still not in traffic. It had been decided when they entered the Works that they would be painted in BR express passenger green but the question of roof colour hadn't been settled, so Simpson, who was known as something of a jester, replied that the hold-up was due to this indecision. 'Freddie', said Harrison, 'You can paint them yellow for all I care, just get them back in service.' In typical fashion, Simpson promptly had the roofs painted primrose yellow. Harrison's reaction is not recorded but within a year the roofs were grey.

The time was well spent, however, and after test workings in multiple with fourteen-coach trains between Derby and Cricklewood, they returned to WCML duties. For a few days in November they hauled the 'Royal Scot' again before being put singly onto such things as Wolverhampton and Birmingham passenger, fitted freight and parcels trains.

The Southern Region's No. 10203 had six-pole traction motors and they were prone to flashover, which is basically a short circuit between the commutator brushes of a DC motor resulting in burning of the commutator. This phenomenon was noted as being more prevalent in cold, damp weather with November being a particularly bad month for it. The other four locomotives – the twins plus SR Nos. 10201 and 10202 – with their four-pole traction motors, were relatively free of the problem until 10000 and 10001 suffered a spate of flashovers after they had been fitted with water pick-up scoops for the train-heating boilers. With 10203's susceptibility to damp weather in mind, it was thought that overflow from the boiler tanks when picking up water could be to

On 4th October 1957, No. 10001 emerged from a light casual repair at Derby Works with the roof painted mid-grey, numbers cream and waist strip eggshell blue except for the portions on the cab and nose doors. The BR crests had been moved above the waist strip, the power classification changed to simply 5, and the lower lining had been removed. I think that it was also during this repair that it was fitted with a water pick-up scoop and the trunking that can be seen emerging from the lower body side and turning underneath between the No. 2 bogie and the battery box. It also had the associated extra roof vents and raised panels above the boiler compartment. In this condition and wearing the altered livery it was photographed entering Birmingham New Street at the head of an express passenger train. COLLECTION REX CONWAY

No. 9 – MAIN LINE DIESEL-ELECTRICS Nos. 10000 and 10001

As the single disc on the lower middle holder indicates, 10000 was running light engine when photographed in late 1957. For a short time after being repainted in this style the previous August, the locomotive retained its 5P 5F power classification but soon after this picture was taken it was changed to 5. R. H. G. SIMPSON

blame. To see what effect overfilling would have, Dennis Monk filled the water tanks on one of the locomotives to capacity and then added a blue aniline dye. Soft asbestos sheets were fitted in front of each leading traction motor and the locomotive taken light engine over Loughborough troughs and back with the scoop down. After the exercise was completed, it was found that only a few spots of blue dye had stained the asbestos sheets and so water contamination from the boiler tank was discounted as a potential cause of flashover.[27] Different grades of carbon were tried for the motor brushes and whilst some improvement was effected, the problems of flashover persisted until eventually they subsided seemingly of their own accord. Some years later, Dennis was riding in the cab of a Metro-Vic locomotive that had suffered three cases of flashover on a type where the problem was previously unknown. When rolling over the viaduct into Manchester Central station, the driver got up from his seat, walked across the cab to collect his bag from the other side and went back to his desk – all without pressing the deadman's override button. He'd managed to do this by putting the master controller into the 'engine only' position and it occurred to Dennis that if he'd inadvertently taken the controller too far and gone into 'reverse', he could have caused a flashover. Whether the practice of going into 'engine only' had become common on 10000 and 10001 and resulted in just such events we will never know, but it is possible.

Fuel cavitation continued to be a problem from time to time, even after the locomotives returned to LMR metals and underwent their lengthy overhaul. On one occasion during September 1956, Dennis Monk was in the cab of 10001 on the 4/15 St. Pancras–Manchester turn when power was lost as the train ascended Sharnbrook bank and speed fell to 25 mph with the controller in notch 8. Suspecting fuel starvation, Dennis and the fireman took it in turns to hand pump fuel up to the service tank and kept the locomotive going to Kettering, where they arrived two minutes late. Examination of the fuel filters at Kettering revealed nothing untoward and after changing the Vokes filter all appeared satisfactory so they continued to Derby, where Dennis left the locomotive to continue to Manchester. The remainder of the journey was uneventful and although no definite reason was found for the trouble, Dennis thinks in retrospect that it was caused by fuel cavitation exacerbated by the gradient at Sharnbrook.

Another recurrent problem was wear and pitting of the fuel pumps. In July 1957, both locomotives were stopped at Willesden for a variety of reasons, one of those on 10001 being very heavy exhaust smoke on full load. Severe pitting, scoured copper washers and worn union nuts were found on the fuel pumps, which had only operated for 100,000 miles since their previous overhaul. The following month the CME's Department informed Bryce Berger that their pumps were not considered satisfactory for rail traction use in their current form and some modifications were suggested. Bryce Berger stated that it would be better to fit an alternative delivery valve assembly with mitre valves and although this was at first considered too expensive, new valves were eventually fitted.

The high spot of the twin diesels' career was 1957 when they ran 126,524 and 130,709 miles respectively on all sorts of turns. These ranged from Euston to Bletchley, Manchester, Birmingham and Wolverhampton trains worked singly to the 'Royal Scot' and West Coast Sleepers in multiple. Although availability in terms of working days showed no improvement over many steam locomotives, weekdays out of service being 106 for 10000 and 102 for 10001, the mileage run was better and the locomotives' utilisation began somewhat to reflect the earlier American experience. The following year was not quite as good because of several failures, including 10001 catching fire at Roade, but mileage was still relatively high at 107,504 and 115,348. The last time they were in charge of the 'Royal Scot' was in April 1958.

From 1959 on, the decline set in. Both locomotives spent more and more time at Derby Works and failures became more common. During the week ending 21st November they were transferred to Willesden. By this time, of course, modernisation plan diesels were entering service in ever-increasing numbers and the LMS twins had gone from being cutting edge British experimental machines to yes-

In early 1958, the locomotives were photographed at Camden coupled together for multiple working. Livery was green with mid-grey roofs, eggshell blue waist strip and cream numbers.
R. S. CARPENTER

On 8th August 1960 No. 10000 entered Derby Works for a heavy casual repair, from which it emerged on 12th November. Six days before officially re-entering traffic, it was photographed outside the Works in its final condition with overhead electrical warning flashes on nose doors and body sides.
MILLBROOK HOUSE, CTY. R. S. CARPENTER

No. 9 — MAIN LINE DIESEL-ELECTRICS Nos. 10000 and 10001

During its final couple of years service, 10000 was used on a variety of secondary duties. This photograph shows it in charge of an ordinary passenger train, unusually indicated by a single lamp rather than a disc, after overhead electrification warning flashes had been applied to the engine compartment doors and left-hand nose doors in 1960. Note that the waist strip sections on cab and nose doors were painted green.
R. H. G. SIMPSON

terday's oddities. In view of the struggle that was taking place to solve the teething problems of the later diesels, the will to keep on top of the troubles besetting a couple of individual locomotives was probably lacking. They were also incompatible with the BR standard diesels for operation in multiple because they had notched controllers rather than infinitely variable ones. Consideration was given to fitting them with later-type control systems but nothing was ever done about it. Utilisation and duties were erratic and the glory days of West Coast Main Line prestige trains were long gone by 1960. Between 19th February and 22nd July that year 10001 went in to Derby Works for another heavy general repair and some rectification was carried out on 10000 in the form of a heavy casual between August and November. After that, relatively little use was made of the locomotives and in 1961 they ran only 32,066 and 37,514 miles respectively.

During 1962 the two diesels achieved even lower mileages and on 26th November, No. 10000 was stored unserviceable in the yard at Derby Works. It never ran again and during the week ending 7th December 1963 was officially withdrawn, having been recorded as running 946,567 miles in fifteen years. It remained in the yard until January 1968

This excellent study of 10001 shows the locomotive at Camden sometime after October 1962. It was in its final condition with yellow nose warning panels and red diamond multiple working markings that can just be discerned above the buffers adjacent to the lower nose door hinges. Overhead electrification warning flashes were present on the body sides above the engine compartment doors and on the left-hand nose doors about halfway up the yellow panels, making them difficult to see in this photograph. Those on 10000 were higher up above the waist strip.
COLLECTION N. E. STEAD

and although I am led to believe that some official consideration was given to preservation, it was then unceremoniously towed away for scrap and cut up by J. Cashmore at Great Bridge the following April.

No. 10001 received a light casual repair between July and October 1962 and with the aid of parts cannibalised from 10000, soldiered on at Willesden employed on various duties, including Willesden–Hither Green cross-London freights, until early 1966. Its utilisation was very poor, however, and during the week ending 12th March that year it was withdrawn with an official 851,151 miles to its credit. Like its twin, 10001 was sold for scrap and was cut up by Cox & Danks of North Acton the following December.

This official LMS photograph was taken when 10000 was first completed and shows it resplendent in black and silver livery with its 'LMS' body side lettering.
BRITISH RAILWAYS LMR, CTY. J. JENNISON

The front end of No. 10000 as built is nicely illustrated in this view of the locomotive about to leave St. Pancras with its first test train on 15th January 1948.
COLLECTION R. J. ESSERY

No. 9 — MAIN LINE DIESEL-ELECTRICS Nos. 10000 and 10001

LIVERY

No. 10001 is shown when new in this study taken at Derby in June 1948. The only difference in livery from 10000 was the absence of bodyside letters.
COLLECTION R. J. ESSERY

When first built, both locomotives were painted gloss black except for the roof, lamp or disc holders, commode handrails, bogies and tyres — which were all painted aluminium colour — and bare metal waist strip, buffers and couplings. Not only the bogie frames, but also the bolsters, beams, springs, brakes, sanding gear and lifeguards were painted aluminium, the axlebox covers being black. Their stock numbers were displayed on each side at either end below the waist strip in LMS 1946 block-style cast-aluminium alloy numerals riveted to the body. No. 10000 had one and a half noughts on the left-hand end cab door of each side and the remainder on the body under the cab side windows. On each right-hand end it had a one and a nought on the cab door. No. 10001 had a nought and a one on each cab door. No. 10000, which had the distinction of being the only LMS locomotive not to be renumbered by British Railways, also had cast-aluminium alloy sans serif 'L M S' letters mounted about halfway between the waist strip and the tumblehome in the centre of each side. The lettering was spaced to fit just inside the inner ends of the bogies and the 'M's split down the middle, each half being mounted on one of the engine compartment doors. No. 10001, being built after Nationalisation, had no such adornment

This picture shows No. 10000 during its early days on the Southern Region in charge of the 4.30 p.m. Bournemouth–Waterloo express. It was wearing the large BR emblems that first had been applied in March 1951 and was without any power classification below the cab side windows. Although it had the extra lamp or disc holders that had been fitted before leaving the LMR, it still lacked those that were added either side of the nose doors above the waist strip. Note how clean the locomotive was with obviously repainted bogies.
B. WEBB, CTY. E. M. JOHNSON

but, somewhat surprisingly, it didn't have 'BRITISH RAILWAYS' either and showed no evidence of ownership. Cast oval makers' plates were fitted to the left-hand ends only of each side between the numbers and the tumblehome forward of the cab doors. The choice of black as the main colour was in keeping with the postwar LMS policy, which was explained by Sir William Wood in a 1946 issue of the LMS staff magazine *Carry On*. The President wrote that touching up was a simple matter with black paint, whereas it was not possible to do satisfactorily with any other colour, and this, together with shortages of paint, painters and cleaners, was responsible for the decision to standardise on black for all locomotives.

The first change of livery occurred when 10000 was repainted in March 1951 following a heavy general repair and although the basic colour scheme remained as before, the large 'L M S' letters were taken off and large-size BR 'monocycling lions'

No. 10000 is seen here at Surbiton sometime between leaving Brighton Works in May 1954 and going back there the following August. It had the extra disc holders, smaller BR emblems and 6P/5F power classification.
COLLECTION REX CONWAY

Below: When the locomotives emerged from their heavy repairs in the late summer of 1956, they were painted in BR locomotive green with primrose yellow roofs and numbers, black and orange lining and everything below the body black, as described in the text. The first to appear in the August was 10001, seen in this official study in its sparkling new livery. In my opinion, it suited the diesels very well.
BRITISH RAILWAYS LMR
CTY. R. J. ESSERY

On 21st September 1956, No. 10000 emerged from Derby Works after a heavy general repair in lined Brunswick green, as described fully in the text, with the small version of 1956 BR crest and the power classification 5P 5F applied to each side. Note the offset of the 5F under the 5P, suggesting that the lower characters were intended to be 5FA. Apparent is the water pick-up trunking between the battery box and the far bogie as well as the raised roof panels above the boiler compartment that were added in October 1955.
COLLECTION D. HILLS

No. 9 – MAIN LINE DIESEL-ELECTRICS Nos. 10000 and 10001

emblems applied below the waist strip. They were positioned between the two ventilation grille panels to the rear of the radiators on the left-hand side and just to the right of the three grilles on the other side. The following month, 10001 appeared in the same livery. In, I think, February and May 1954 respectively, the large transfers were replaced on both locomotives by the smaller variety placed centrally in the lower panels of the engine compartment doors nearer to No. 2 end. At the same time, the power classification 6P/5F was stencilled in 2in scroll and serif characters forward of the cab doors between the aluminium alloy numbers and the waist strip on both locomotives. No. 10001 retained this until its return to the LMR but 10000 later received 6P 5FA in 2in cream Gill Sans transfers.

In August and September 1956 the two locomotives were repainted at Derby Works in Brunswick green with everything below the tumblehome black and buffer fairings signal red. Roofs and numbers were primrose yellow, courtesy of Freddie Simpson's sense of humour, whilst buffers and couplings remained bare metal. The waist strips were lined with a one inch wide black line along the centre flanked by ½ inch green lines with ¼ inch orange edging. Similar lining was applied along the lower edge of the body immediately above the tumblehome and running all the way around the locomotive. The smaller version of the then new BR crest was applied to each side below the waist strip and between the engine compartment ventilation grilles adjacent to the radiators. The lions on the right-hand sides were the early, heraldically incorrect, right-facing ones. The power classification on 10001 was shown in 2in cream Gill Sans transfers as 5P 5FA placed between the waist strip and the middle zero of the stock number, the 5P being centrally above the 5FA. No. 10000, however, showed 5P 5F, although the characters were staggered with the upper 5 above the F and it looked as though it too was intended to have been 5P 5FA. The shed code of 1A was painted in cream Gill Sans characters on the nose to the left of the door when looking forwards and just below the lower hinge bracket. The makers' plates had polished characters on a black background.

In August 1957, No. 10000 emerged from Derby Works with its roof painted mid-grey, numbers cream and waist strip eggshell blue apart from the sections on the cab and nose doors, which were green. The crests, with the correct left-facing lions on both sides, had been moved above the waist strip between the side windows towards the No. 2 end and the power classification was simply 5. Just over a month later, No. 10001 was in the same livery. A short while later the power classification was reduced to simply 5.

At least one report suggests that at some stage the waist strip sections on the cab doors and nose doors of 10000 were bare aluminium alloy but I have no further information. In 1960, overhead electrification warning flashes were applied above the engine compartment doors and on the left-hand nose doors and in 1961, the waist strip on 10001 was eggshell blue all round including the cab and nose door portions. Probably coincidental with that, cast 1A shed plates were fitted to both locomotives at the left-hand ends just above the makers' plates. Colour photographs after this time show 10001's numbers to have been painted white but I don't know exactly when this was done. In October 1962, No. 10001 had the small type of yellow warning panels painted on the nose at each end. At some stage in the 1960s, red diamonds were painted on the noses for multiple working indication but I can't state exactly when.

This study of 10001, taken at Willesden in 1962, is one of the few to show the cast 1A shed plates that were fitted to both 10000 and 10001 in 1961. One of the plates can be seen quite clearly between the makers' plate and number at the end nearer the camera. R. H. G. SIMPSON

This excellent study illustrates 10001 in its final condition prior to withdrawal. Livery was BR green with eggshell blue waist strip, including the portions on cab and nose doors, white numbers and yellow nose panels with red diamonds on them above the buffers. Overhead warning flashes had been applied, those on the left-hand nose doors being below the waist strip, and fairings over the buffer housings were red. Grab handles had been fitted to the corners of the nose sections on the waist strips and to the nose doors just above the strips. The raised panels on the roof that were fitted along with water pick-up apparatus are evident just behind the cab at the near end and the trunking from pick-up scoop to train-heating boiler water tank can be seen just behind the near bogie. R. H. G. SIMPSON

CONCLUSIONS

So what did the LMS main-line diesel-electric experiment achieve? Initially it showed that Sir Harold Hartley and Fairburn had been right when they doubted that the huge first cost could be recovered in savings due to increased availability and mileage. Certainly up to the early 1950s, they were definitely not worth the extra outlay in purely economic terms and the 'dieselisation' of British Railways didn't happen as soon as many of those involved with the introduction of the LMS locomotives had hoped. As the cost of labour and coal increased and quality of the latter decreased even further, however, the pendulum began to swing. Even so, the first large-scale introduction of diesel traction, apart from shunters, was in the form of multiple units – a situation probably foretold by the pre-war experiments of the LMS and others. They did show that the other potential advantages identified by Ivatt in 1946 – improved availability, better scheduling and less smoke and dirt – were definitely attainable given the right environment.

One of the more obvious legacies was that much experience was gained, albeit on a limited scale, that was of great value when the modernisation plan diesels were being designed and put into service. The considerations and machinations of the period surrounding the various modernisation plans, establishment and dissolution of the Railway Executive, and establishment of the Transport Commission are fiendishly complex and way outside a publication such as this – even if I could produce a convincing résumé. Whether or not 'dieselisation' was or was not a wise move is still argued but the fact is that it happened and when it did, there were benefits accruing from the 10000/10001 experience.[28]

For example, there was a faction in BR that wanted to concentrate diesel production on relatively small standard units, thus saving on design and construction costs, spares holding and maintenance when compared with the provision of several different types. When the need arose for greater power, two or more units could be coupled together as was the practice on some American railroads. After all, steam locomotives were double-headed on many occasions and with diesels the cost of a second crew would be avoided. The studies on initial cost undertaken when the LMS diesel-electrics were being considered, together with the ascertained costs of operating them in multiple, however, showed that the overall financial burden of two or more units was substantially more than that of a single, more powerful locomotive. This had a direct bearing on BR's diesel acquisition policy. Experience of operating the LMS locomotives had also given a lot of data on component and system reliability, maintainability and robustness. This was invaluable when ordering and/or designing the next generation of diesels, even though the lessons on train heating seem to have been missed. Some of the better mechanical details and aspects of such things as bogie design were carried on into subsequent classes and it was no accident that the Derby diesels of later years had a strong family resemblance in many ways. Classes 44, 45 and 46 all had a direct lineage to 10000 and 10001. The bogie design in particular was excellent and was used almost unaltered in the Class 77 EM2 electrics.

One of the more notable benefits accrued not to British Railways directly but through English Electric. The experience they gained from 10000 and 10001, as well as the Southern trio, was put to good effect and later English Electric designs such as the Class 40 and very successful Class 37 diesel-electrics owed much to it. Again, some of Derby's design details were utilised. The 16SVT engine was steadily improved, achieving 2,000 hp in the Class 40s, 2,700 hp in the Class 50s and 3,250 hp in the Class 56s.

Other lessons included the need for a much cleaner maintenance environment than existed at steam sheds and that centralisation of maintenance effort for all except minor occurrences, as was effectively done with steam locomotives, was not cost-effective for diesels. The need for proper education and training for footplate crews and maintenance staff was also highlighted and the areas of greatest need identified. It is regrettable, of course, that one of the major lessons was concerned with train heating but that was effectively ignored, which did BR untold harm in the 1960s.

But what of the locomotives themselves? How successful can they be said to have been apart from their legacy to future generations? Considering the speed with which they were conceived, designed and built with little data or experience for guidance, I think that they were outstanding machines. Whilst it would be silly to claim that they didn't suffer from annoying faults and were sometimes prone to failures, many of the problems experienced with them were more due to circumstances than to the locomotives themselves. For most of their lives, their maintenance facilities were not purpose-built but were adapted within what was a fairly hostile environment for technologically advanced machines. There was also, whether it is admitted or not, a degree of antipathy in many quarters towards what some people saw as nuisances. As their performance in 1950 and 1951 showed though, even without proper support they were capable of a good showing and when they received the right attention in 1957 and 1958 they began to achieve what I suspect was getting on towards their true potential. After that, they reverted to being oddities whose control systems were incompatible with standard BR diesels and which many saw as intrusions, so they were basically allowed to rot. Even so, they lasted longer than some later diesel classes and for true pioneers, that can't be a bad epitaph. Dennis Monk examined 10000 when she was stored outside Derby No. 2 shed by what was known as 'Pickering's Pit' between 1963 and 1968 and says that there was no sign of any cracking or deterioration of the bogie frames, which in itself is remarkable.[29]

The fact also remains that they were the first of their kind – the pioneer British main-line diesel-electrics, destined to be the forerunners of machines that would take over vast tracts of the British Railways network and sweep away the steam locomotive. With that in mind and considering the diesel types that have been rescued from extinction and maintained for posterity in working order, it seems a great shame that neither of these groundbreaking machines was saved from the breaker's torch.

NOTES IN TEXT

1. The often-made assertion that it was the first British main-line diesel locomotive is not quite true. In 1934, Armstrong Whitworth had built an 800 hp 1-Co-1 main-line diesel demonstrator that was used on the LNER for limited freight and passenger workings.
2. The Midland electrified its Lancaster, Morecambe and Heysham line in 1908 but it wasn't really successful, whereas the L&NWR's conversion to electric traction for the intensive London suburban traffic out to Watford was. The short L&YR branch from Bury to Holcombe Brook was electrified for a brief time in 1913 by Dick, Kerr & Co. at their own expense in order to gain experience with the system. The L&YR Manchester-Bury commuter route was converted by the railway company itself. The Midland Railway was considering electrification of the Birmingham-Bristol route over the Lickey Incline before the first world war but hostilities intervened and the scheme wasn't resurrected after 1918. In 1923 there was a proposal to electrify the West Coast Main Line between Crewe and Carlisle and some preliminary work, including diagrams of possible locomotives, was undertaken but there was no Board approval and the whole scheme was abandoned in 1924. The Weir report of 1931 recommended that the plan would be worth pursuing but the necessary funds could not be obtained. Also in 1931, the Manchester, South Junction & Altrincham Railway, a busy commuter line jointly owned before the Grouping by the L&YR and Great Central and passed into the hands of the LMS and L&NER, was also electrified. In 1936, the LMS considered electrifying the main line from Euston to Rugby but the economics were against it. The last part of the LMS to be electrified before Nationalisation, in 1938, was the Wirral Railway that connected at Birkenhead Park with the Mersey Railway, which had itself been electrified as far back as 1903.
3. The LNER also used Sentinel railcars and seems to have had more success with them, or at least found them more acceptable, than the LMS did.
4. This was largely the result of statistical analysis instigated by Stamp as part of his drive for economy. Records showed that no less than half the working hours booked to goods engines were spent shunting and it became apparent that great savings were potentially possible in this area.
5. In this context I am referring to spark or bulb-ignition oil engines rather than compression-ignition types.
6. There were actually a great many more transmission systems that were the subjects of experimentation and development. They included hydrokinetic, hydromechanical and hydrostatic – all variations on hydraulic transmission – as well as direct drive, compressed air, compressed gas and compressed steam systems. None, however, was sufficiently advanced to be seriously considered when the LMS was deciding which method to use.
7. This was the set that had run on the Bury to Holcombe Brook branch when the route was electrified for a brief time in 1913 by Dick, Kerr & Co. See note 2 above.
8. Beardmore engines were undoubtedly ahead of their time and it is to be regretted that the type didn't meet with more acceptance, particularly in the UK. They were made in various sizes from 90 to 1,330 hp running at between 800 and 1,200 rpm. Unfortunately, their production was only a minor part of the Beardmore Group's activities and in 1934 it was decided to discontinue them as the economic climate worsened. It is somewhat ironic that from this date, interest in the lightweight, fast-running diesel engine started to grow exponentially across the world.
9. Further details of that locomotive can be found in Phil Chopping's article in *LMS Journal No. 2* published by Wild Swan.
10. Apart from the diesels, six Sentinel 0-4-0T shunters were obtained between 1930 and 1934. The first three were delivered in 1930 and were two-cylinder, chain-drive locomotives. Their power output was limited and although they lasted until Nationalisation, no further examples were purchased. A smaller version was built in 1931 and taken into stock in 1932 specifically for working the Clee Hill Quarries in Shropshire. In November 1934, an experimental, oil-fired Doble boiler compound Sentinel 0-4-0T was bought for comparison with the early diesel shunters but showed no advantage over conventional steam shunters so the order for a second one was cancelled.
11. Some of these machines were ordered by the LMS whereas others underwent trials before being bought by the company. For further details see *An Illustrated History of LMS Locomotives Volume 5* by Essery and Jenkinson published by Silver Link Publishing.
12. Strange to relate, the next time a dual braking system featured in a British diesel locomotive was 1963.
13. There were other factors in the failure of the diesel-hydraulic locomotive to impress and I again refer interested readers to Phil Chopping's article in *LMS Journal No. 2*.
14. The English Electric locomotives were the direct forebears of the highly successful British Railways Class 8 diesel shunters known to enthusiasts as 'Gronks'. Hornbuckle remained faithful to the cause of mechanical transmission and his view was partly justified when British Railways put into service a successful range of lower-powered diesel-mechanical shunters many years later. In 1953 and 1954, Horwich Works built five 0-4-0ST steam shunters for BR based on a Kitson design that had been sold on the LMS, five having been bought in 1932.
15. For example, an LMS Pacific and a 'Deltic' were both capable of similar maximum power output and of hauling 500 ton trains on the level at about 90 mph. Whereas it would take the steam locomotive about seventeen minutes to attain that speed, however, the diesel would take just four minutes. This would represent about a 4½ minute saving over the first twenty miles run.
16. The Whyte system of notation for locomotive wheel arrangements is not as suitable for diesel and electric locomotives as the UIC system based originally on German practice. For anyone not familiar with the UIC system, powered axles are indicated by letters and unpowered ones by numbers. A indicates a single powered axle, B is two powered axles together, C is three and D is four. Where axles in a group are powered by individual electric motors, this is indicated by an 'o' suffix. Thus, an A1A-A1A would have had two bogies, each with three axles. The outer axles of each bogie would have been powered but the intermediate ones unpowered. A locomotive of 1A-Bo-A1 layout would have had two four wheeled bogies, each having an unpowered axle and a powered axle, with two powered axles in the frames between them, each with its own traction motor. A Do-Do would have had two bogies, each with four powered axles. Nos. 10000 and 10001 were Co-Cos, so had two bogies with three powered axles each.
17. The English Electric Company was formed in 1918 by the amalgamation of Dick, Kerr & Co. Ltd of Preston, Phoenix Dynamo & Manufacturing Co. of Bradford, Siemens Bros. Ltd. of Stafford, and Willans & Robinson Ltd. of Rugby. In 1955 it took over the Vulcan Foundry of Newton-le-Willows and Robert Stephenson & Hawthorns of Newcastle then, in 1961, it also absorbed W. G. Bagnall Ltd. of Stafford.
18. It would appear that the intention to compare directly the diesels with the improved Pacifics wasn't pursued following Nationalisation. Certainly, I have yet to see any reports or reference to such trials.
19. Research into pulverised coal-fuelled gas-turbine traction was funded by the six largest coal-carrying railroads and the three largest coal producers in America. It was mainly carried out by a research team from Johns Hopkins University.
20. The LNER and Southern were also considering the introduction of diesels. Only the latter, however, proceeded with them.
21. There were two power classification systems in use on British Railways – statistical, which was used by the Motive Power Department to indicate haulage capacity, and loading, which was used by the Operating Department and included braking power. The Southern Region displayed the loading classification on its locomotives whereas all other regions used statistical classification – hence the difference when locomotives went to and from the Southern.
22. The 16SVT was capable of running at 850 rpm, at which speed it could produce 2,000 hp – as was done on the Southern Region's No. 10203. For LMS purposes, however, it was decided to limit it to 750 rpm.
23. Continuous weak field rating of the traction motors was actually 220 hp at 300 volts and 550 amps but they were installed to work at the figures quoted.
24. There was a suggestion early in the design stage that standard coaching stock corridor connections should be used. This would have presented several difficulties, not least of which were the cab layout and visibility, and the idea was dropped.
25. For more details on the progressive repair system used by the LMS, see *Locomotives Repairs on the LMS* by the same author in *LMS Journal No. 8* published by Wild Swan.
26. The three Southern region main-line diesels also spent a lot of time at Derby Works during 1956.
27. As an amusing aside to this trial, as the locomotive approached the troughs on the outward trip, the driver whistled to warn the permanent way gang working there. The gang stood back but didn't go as far away as they would have at the approach of a steam locomotive – after all, it was a diesel and diesels, especially those without a train, didn't pick up water, did they? Despite repeated hooting, the gang stood by the track side and waited for the locomotive to pass. On the return trip, Dennis noticed the PW gang well back from the troughs with their jackets all hanging on the fence to dry!
28. The fact that the original BR modernisation plan envisaged steam giving way directly to electric traction, with diesels being mainly confined to shunting and other lesser duties, is outside the scope of this book. It must be remembered, however, that conditions had changed by 1955 and that the entire, Government-controlled national rail system was being considered as a whole. Gas turbines were tried to a very limited extent in the mid-1950s but sufficient funding for a meaningful assessment was not provided.
29. 'Pickering's Pit' was christened after Joseph Pickering, a driver who joined the Midland in 1845 and was blamed for a collision at Knighton Junction in 1854. As a result, he was taken off main-line duties and put onto testing engines coming out of Derby Works following repair. Before running trials with them, Joe and the fitters would attend to small defects and setting of the springs outside No. 2 shed. He remained at Derby until 1882, the area where he worked becoming known ever after as 'Pickering's Pit'.

APPENDICES
APPENDIX A – TABLES OF VISIBLE ALTERATIONS

In order to assist modellers and artists who wish to portray the LMS main-line diesel-electrics at a particular time in their lives, I have included the accompanying tables showing the main alterations to them visible from outside. Dates are those on which, to the best of my knowledge, the locomotives appeared in traffic with the alterations incorporated, those with asterisks being probable dates of which I can't be certain.

No. 10000

Date of alteration	Description
22nd September 1948	Extra stiffening webs fitted to bogie side plates. Oval access panels to boiler fuel & water tanks filled in.
2nd May 1949	Valance between buffers removed and jumper connectors permanently fitted.
9th March 1951	Raised aluminium alloy 'L M S' letters removed from sides. Large size BR emblems applied – see text for positioning.
24th February 1953	Cab handrails and grille panels trimmed back. Extra lamp or disc holders fitted to nose sections just below waist strip above buffers and electric lights installed next to them.
5th May 1954*	Large BR emblems replaced by smaller variety and 6P/ 5F power classification added – see text for positioning. Two more lamp or disc holders fitted either side of nose doors. Power classification later changed to 6P 5FA – date unknown.
13th October 1955	Water pick-up trunking from scoop to lower body sides fitted between bogie and battery box at No. 2 end. Raised roof panels fitted at either side above boiler compartment.
21st September 1956	Lamp or disc holders either side of nose doors removed. Repainted Brunswick green. Everything below tumblehome black, roof and numbers primrose yellow. Waist strip and lower part of body lined orange/green/black/green/orange. Smaller version of 1956 BR crest applied to each side. Power classification 5P 5F applied. See text for full details.
29th August 1957	Roof painted mid-grey, numbers cream and waist strip eggshell blue. Crests moved, power classification changed to 5, and lower lining removed. Waist strip sections on cab doors and nose doors green but possibly bare aluminium alloy later. See text for full details.
1960	Overhead electrification warning flashes applied. Red diamonds painted on nose section*.

No. 10001

Date of alteration	Description
10th April 1951	Large size BR emblems applied – see text for positioning.
17th April 1953	Cab handrails and grille panels trimmed back. Extra lamp or disc holders fitted to nose sections just below waist strip above buffers and electric lights installed next to them.
15th February 1954*	Large BR emblems replaced by smaller variety and 6P/5F power classification added – see text for positioning. Two more lamp or disc holders fitted either side of nose doors.
24th August 1956	Repainted Brunswick green. Everything below tumblehome black, roof and numbers primrose yellow. Waist strip and lower part of body lined orange/green/black/green/orange. Smaller version of 1956 BR crest applied to each side. Power classification 5P 5FA applied. See text for full details. Lamp or disc holders either side of nose doors removed.
4th October 1957	Roof painted mid-grey, numbers cream and waist strip eggshell blue – portions on cab and nose doors green. Crests moved, power classification changed to 5, and lower lining removed. See text for full details. Raised roof panels fitted at either side above boiler compartment*. Water pick-up trunking from scoop to lower body sides fitted between bogie and battery box at No. 2 end*.
1960	Overhead electrification warning flashes applied. Red diamonds painted on nose section*.
1961	Grab handles fitted to corners of nose sections on waist strips and to nose doors just above strips. Cab and nose door portions of waist strip painted eggshell blue. Numbers painted white*.
27th October 1962	Small yellow warning panels painted on nose sections. Buffer fairings painted red.

APPENDIX B – SERVICE DETAILS

Official shed allocations were as follows:

10000
- 13 Dec 47 – Camden
- 20 Dec 47 – Derby (loan)
- 9 Oct 48 – Camden
- 13 Nov 48 – Willesden
- 22 Jan 49 – Derby (loan)
- 28 May 49 – Willesden
- 7 Mar 53 – Nine Elms
- 16 Apr 55 – Camden
- 21 Nov 59 – Willesden

10001
- 19 Jul 48 – Camden
- 24 Jul 48 – Derby (loan)
- 9 Oct 48 – Camden
- 13 Nov 48 – Willesden
- 22 Jan 49 – Derby (loan)
- 28 May 49 – Willesden
- 25 Apr 53 – Nine Elms
- 12 Mar 55 – Camden
- 21 Nov 59 – Willesden

Dates when the engines were *officially* out of service were as follows:

10000
- 2 Aug–22 Sep 48
- 9 Oct 48–1 Feb 49
- 2 Feb–2 May 49
- 13 Mar–1 May 50
- 2–8 May 50
- 14–17 Jul 50
- 28 Nov 50–9 Mar 51
- 16 Jun–13 Jul 51
- 4 Jan–15 Feb 52
- 9 Jun–3 Jul 52
- 15 Sep–3 Oct 52
- 8 Dec 52–24 Feb 53
- 5 Oct 53–5 May 54
- 26 Aug 54–25 Feb 55
- 12 Mar–1 Apr 55
- 25 Aug – 13 Oct 55
- 21 Oct –4 Nov 55
- 7 Jan–21 Sep 56
- 27 Dec 56–11 Jan 57
- 8–28 Mar 57
- 30 Jul –29 Aug 57
- 19 Sep–15 Oct 57
- 11–13 Dec 57
- 12 Mar–25 Apr 58
- 17 May–16 Jun 58
- 29 Aug –12 Sep 58
- 2 Jan–13 Feb 59
- 19 Jan–17 Mar 60
- 8 Aug–12 Nov 60
- 1 Feb–10 Mar 61
- No further information available until stored out of use from 26 Nov 62–7 Dec 63. Locomotive then withdrawn.

10001
- 9 Aug–9 Sep 48
- 9 Oct 48–8 Jan 49
- 8–11 Feb 49
- 5–8 Apr 49
- 5–21 May 49
- 11 Nov 49–7 Mar 50
- 14–17 Jul 50
- 28 Nov 50–10 Apr 51
- 16–21 Jun 51
- 7–14 Sep 51
- 14 Nov 51–16 Jan 52
- 3 Oct–7 Nov 52
- 21 Jan–17 Apr 53
- 29 Jun 53–15 Feb 54
- 22 Apr –19 May 54
- 17–29 Jun 54
- 27 Jul –19 Aug 54
- 6 Sep –8 Oct 54
- 20 Oct –8 Nov 54
- 14–29 Dec 54
- 14 Feb –4 Mar 55
- 16 Jun–16 Sep 55
- 20 Oct – 16 Dec 55
- 8 Jan–24 Aug 56
- 4 Feb–7 Mar 57
- 29 May–5 Jun 57
- 27 Aug–4 Oct 57
- 6–14 Jan 58
- 12–21 Mar 58
- 13 May–12 Jun 58
- 22 Jan–13 Mar 59
- 25 Jun–10 Jul 59
- 19 Feb–22 Jul 60
- 12 Jul–27 Oct 62
- No further information until withdrawal in week ending 12 Mar 66.